RUTGERS UNIVERSITY STUDIES IN ENGLISH
NUMBER ONE

SHAKESPEARE'S INFLUENCE
ON THE DRAMA OF HIS AGE

Shakespeare's Influence on the Drama of his Age

STUDIED IN *HAMLET*

By

DONALD JOSEPH McGINN

OCTAGON BOOKS

A DIVISION OF FARRAR, STRAUS AND GIROUX

New York   1973

Reprinted 1965
by special arrangement with Rutgers University Press

Second Octagon printing 1973

OCTAGON BOOKS
A DIVISION OF FARRAR, STRAUS & GIROUX, INC.
19 Union Square West
New York, N. Y. 10003

LIBRARY OF CONGRESS CATALOG CARD NUMBER: 65-25884
ISBN 0-374-95510-7

Printed in U.S.A. by
NOBLE OFFSET PRINTERS, INC.
NEW YORK, N.Y. 10003

TO MY MOTHER

CONTENTS

PREFACE

EVERY student of the English dramatic literature from 1600 to 1642 has undoubtedly discovered occasional imitations of Shakespeare in the plays of his contemporaries. And it is hardly strange that a playwright extremely popular with the audiences in the theatres of his own time should be imitated by other writers attempting to please that public. Yet some scholars to-day seem uncertain of the extent and importance of Shakespeare's influence on his fellow dramatists. Bonamy Dobrée, for example, writes, "To what degree he was influenced by his collaborators, how much effect he had on them, is a dubious matter."[1] Then, referring more specifically to the tragedy of revenge, of which *Hamlet* is the most famous representative, Professor Dobrée altogether discounts Shakespeare's influence: "Indeed on one outstanding point, the treatment of the revenge motive, his work appears to have had no effect, for its disintegration in *Hamlet* put no stop to the theme in all its crudeness, as we see from Chapman and Tourneur."[2] Professor E. E. Stoll even more emphatically states that "although more than twenty years in London Shakespeare seems to have made no stir," for "in his own day, nobody of real importance, save Webster . . . took public notice of his merits as a playwright at all."[3]

[1] *A Companion to Shakespeare Studies* ed. by Harley Granville-Barker and G. B. Harrison, 1934, p. 259.

[2] *Ibid.*, p. 260.

[3] *Shakespeare Studies*, 1927, p. 6.

Perhaps the fear of seeming to idolize the man whom succeeding generations have pronounced the greatest English playwright may have prevented a satisfactory estimate of Shakespeare's influence in his own day. Be that as it may, convinced that such an estimate has not been made, I am selecting as a criterion of the Poet's reputation among his contemporaries a play which to-day receives universal acclaim—that very play, indeed, the early effect of which Professor Dobrée especially discounts—namely, *Hamlet*. The greatest obstacle in the way of a true judgment of the importance of *Hamlet*, it seems to me, is the misunderstanding of its relation to another tragedy of revenge closely resembling it, *Antonio's Revenge* by John Marston. In this book I present additional evidence in support of my conviction, elsewhere more fully expressed,[1] that the author of *Antonio's Revenge* was indebted to Shakespeare both for plot and for characterization. Then in order to show the importance of *Hamlet* merely as a revenge-play I discuss at length its relation to other plays of the same type written before 1642. Finally, I trace its influence on the remaining dramatic literature of the period.

My most difficult task has been to distinguish the imitations of *Hamlet* from dramatic devices that may have been employed by every playwright of the time. As far as the conventions of the tragedy of revenge are concerned, however, I am fortunate in that so many able scholars have already defined them so clearly that there is little chance of their being confused with purely Shakespearean innovations. For example, Dr. A. H. Thorndike's study of the relation of *Hamlet* to con-

---

[1] *PMLA*, LIII (March, 1938), pp. 129-37.

temporary revenge-plays[1] I have found most enlighten-
ing, though I am unable to agree with many of his
conclusions. In addition, from two theses now in the
Cornell University Library—*The Tragedy of Revenge*
by Miss Rose Alden and *Shakespearean Characters and
Situations in Beaumont and Fletcher, Ford, Massinger,
and Marston* by Miss Grace E. Cornelius—I have derived
several suggestions valuable for this study.

But other imitations of character and scene in *Hamlet*,
not bearing directly on the revenge-motif, have been
less easy to distinguish. In most instances a similarity of
phrasing first attracted my attention to the particular
imitation. As a result, almost every imitation of character or scene cited is accompanied by verbal echoes.
These verbal allusions represent the most delicate part
of my investigation. Some readers may accuse me of
not including all the echoes of *Hamlet* that occurred in
the period under observation. Others may feel that I
have included too many. For the benefit of both let
me point out that only a fraction of my original collection appears in the 474 verbal allusions recorded in
Part Two of this book. These I have weighed so care-
fully that I might decide on Monday to incorporate
certain of them in my study, on Wednesday to remove
them, and on Saturday to replace them. Yet had I taken
them all, I should have done little more than reinforce
my present argument, for a large part of the discarded
allusions come from plays of Beaumont and Fletcher,
Marston, Massinger, and Ford, whose debt is already
fairly obvious. On the contrary, the more skeptical may
remove, if they will, at least a hundred—I hardly believe

[1] *PMLA*, XVII, (1902), pp. 125-220.

that they will deem it necessary to take more—and still Shakespeare's influence on his fellow playwrights will be manifest; indeed, there will remain well over three hundred allusions not hitherto recorded.

My chief purpose in writing this preface, however, is not so much to explain the aims of my book as to express my gratitude to the friends whose help has made it possible. Without the generous assistance of Dr. Joseph Q. Adams, now Director of the Folger Shakespeare Library, I should never have undertaken the task. His admirable lectures of a decade ago at Cornell University, characterized as they were by imagination balanced by sound common sense, first aroused my interest in Shakespeare. Furthermore, Dr. Adams not only suggested the subject for study, but twice read my manuscript, each time giving valuable advice. I may also add that I have adopted without reservation his interpretation of *Hamlet*, as set forth in the Commentary in his excellent edition of that play. Whatever of lasting importance may be in this work, then, I attribute to him whose name I honor "on this side idolatry as much as any."

To another former teacher, Professor Lane Cooper of Cornell University, an alumnus of Rutgers, I also desire to express my gratitude, not only for reading my manuscript, but more particularly for revealing to me his high ideal of the importance of scholarly work in the life of the teacher, in striving to attain to which I have written this book.

Professor Herbert A. Wichelns, also of Cornell, with his keen analytical mind, perceived many of the flaws in logical presentation in my study in its earlier stages, and has thus doubtless saved me much humiliation. My colleague, Professor Rudolf Kirk, has rendered valuable assistance quite as much with his friendly encouragement as by reading my manuscript.

The Cornell and Rutgers University libraries have placed at my disposal their excellent collections of the Elizabethan dramatists. I am particularly grateful to Mr. George A. Osborn, the librarian of Rutgers University, and to his assistant, Miss Edith Deerr, who have exerted every effort to provide me with the necessary texts; also to Miss Catherine Waguette, another of Mr. Osborn's assistants, whose suggestions regarding bibliography I have incorporated in my work.

DONALD JOSEPH McGINN

New Brunswick, New Jersey
May, 1938

SHAKESPEARE'S INFLUENCE
ON THE DRAMA OF HIS AGE

PART ONE

My *Shakespeare*, rise; I will not lodge thee by
 Chaucer, or *Spenser*, or bid *Beaumont* lye
A little further, to make thee a roome:
 Thou art a Moniment, without a tombe,
And art alive still, while thy Booke doth live,
 And we have wits to read, and praise to give.
That I not mixe thee so, my braine excuses;
 I meane with great, but disproportion'd *Muses*,
For, if I thought my judgement were of yeeres,
 I should commit thee surely with thy peeres,
And tell, how farre thou didst our *Lily* out-shine,
 Or sporting *Kid*, or *Marlowes* mighty line.

Ben Jonson

I

THE TOUCHSTONE

AS AN essential part of our culture, *Hamlet* ranks almost as high as the English Bible. The unconscious borrowings from it, both in our conversation and in our contemporary literature, reveal even more than do deliberate quotations the depths of its impression on our thought. Regarding its vast influence during its existence of over three hundred years, Mr. John Munro writes in *The Shakspere Allusion-Book*:[1]

> From no other play of Shakespeare's, probably from no other similar composition in the world, have so many phrases been borrowed, and of no other, probably, have so many passages and scenes been imitated.

It is not surprising, therefore, that many people ascribe its present fame to three centuries of praise. Before accepting this explanation, however, we should first ascertain the reputation of the play shortly after its initial presentation on the English stage. Was it so highly regarded by Shakespeare's contemporaries? The answer to our question appears, in part, in *The Shakspere Allusion-Book*, which reveals that *Hamlet* is the source of forty-three per cent of all the allusions to Shakespeare's plays before the year 1642. It is thus evident that in the golden age of English drama the tragedy exerted a strong appeal.

[1] *The Shakspere Allusion-Book: A Collection of Allusions to Shakspere from 1591 to 1700*, 1909, I, p. xxiv.

The *Allusion-Book* presents the only study hitherto made of the influence of *Hamlet* on the seventeenth century; yet even a cursory glance at the plays written before 1642 arouses the suspicion that the work records but a small share of the references to the tragedy in this early period. Though the allusions recorded, forty-five in all, far outnumber those to any other play, they are woefully incomplete, for in only one or two instances do they extend beyond brief passages containing either the name of the play or an echo of some familiar line; in short, they are mere verbal allusions. For example, in Beaumont and Fletcher's *Philaster*, the hero of which, like Hamlet, has "cause, and will, and strength, and means" to avenge the usurpation of his father's throne but cannot act, Mr. Munro neglects all resemblance of character and plot; he finds, indeed, only one allusion—an echo of Claudius' prayer.[1] From John Marston's *Insatiate Countess* he again selects a single passage; and then in a footnote, mentioning a second allusion that was not admitted to an earlier collection, he concludes with a brief quotation from A. H. Bullen, "There are heaps of echoes from *Hamlet* in this play."[2] He also might well have called attention to the resemblance in the play between Countess Isabella and Queen Gertrude. But most indicative of the sketchy nature of the *Allusion-Book* as far as *Hamlet* is concerned is the treatment of the plays of William Heminge, from which only two allusions are extracted, both from *The Jewes Tragedy*, whereas *The Fatal Contract*, packed with borrowings, is not even mentioned.

[1] *Ibid.*, I, p. 196. See also p. xlii.
[2] *Ibid.*, I, p. 236 n.

Apparently realizing the shortcomings of his work, Mr. Munro warns the reader that the "imitation of scenes is a field which has not yet been sufficiently explored," and adds that he suspects the possibility of the existence of "many more cases than those hitherto discovered."[1] Without searching for these "cases," however, he designates *Hamlet* one of the four dramatic works upon which Shakespeare's contemporary reputation was founded; in fact, he goes so far as to state that "evidences of the play's profound influence are to be seen, not in the ordinary verbal allusions, but in the many imitations and plagiarisings,"[2] which he considers the greatest testimony of all to Shakespeare's superiority over his fellow poets and playwrights.

In spite of this statement he somewhat inconsistently asserts that Shakespeare left no school behind him:

> He was not an initiator; he invented no new style; he introduced no new vogue . . . Both Marlowe and Kyd left behind them types which long served for models; the romantic plays of Beaumont and Fletcher continued to exercise a wide influence over the stage; but it was long before the works of Shakespeare were considered as models which playwrights might profitably study. We shall not expect to find, therefore, in Jacobean and post-Jacobean drama up to the Restoration, any evidence of plays on a Shakespearean model.[3]

Mr. Munro thus faces a dilemma: he admits the influence of the play but not of its author. Since, then,

[1] *Ibid.*, I, p. xliv. The borrowings from the ghost scenes recorded in the *Allusion-Book* are hardly more than verbal echoes. The only extensive imitation of scene noted by Munro is the graveyard scene in *The Jealous Lovers* (*ibid.*, I, p. xli).

[2] *Ibid.*, I, p. xxiv.

[3] *Ibid.*, I, p. xxxiv.

the evidence of the *Allusion-Book* is incomplete and the conclusions of its editor are contradictory, I purpose to select *Hamlet*, and apply it as a sort of touchstone to subsequent plays written before the closing of the theatres. By this test I hope to reveal something of the nature and extent of Shakespeare's reputation among his contemporaries.

The quest for the influence of *Hamlet* on the dramatic literature of England from 1600 to 1642 is at the very outset impeded by the presence of another *Hamlet* familiar to Elizabethan playwrights for at least a decade before the Shakespearean version. Indeed, without the aid of Dr. Joseph Q. Adams' exhaustive study of its sources and history,[1] I should have been much handicapped in my efforts to distinguish between allusions to the play as we now know it and the lost original. According to Dr. Adams, the *Ur-Hamlet* probably appeared about 1589, for in an epistle prefixed to Robert Greene's *Menaphon* (1589), Thomas Nashe alludes to Thomas Kyd, the foremost playwright of the day, with the apparent aim of censuring Kyd's imitation of Senecan tragedy: "He will afford you whole *Hamlets*—I should say handfuls of tragical speeches."[2] The only surviving vestiges of the original tragedy appear in the *Fratricide*

---

[1] *Hamlet*, 1929, pp. 335 ff.

[2] *Ibid.*, p. 340. Dr. Adams warns us that this allusion of Nashe might be construed to refer either to Kyd or to a slavish imitator; yet he points out that the close resemblance between *Hieronimo* (*The Spanish Tragedy*) and the early *Hamlet* as we know it through the *Fratricide Punished* and the pirated quarto of 1603 has satisfied most authorities that Kyd wrote the *Ur-Hamlet*.

Punished (Der Bestrafte Brudermord oder Prinz Hamlet aus Daennemark) and the pirated First Quarto of 1603.[1]

The *Fratricide Punished* represents a German transcript of the play in this early stage. Professor J. Dover Wilson considers it "at least possible that its derivation belongs to a date before that at which Shakespeare's *Hamlet* took final shape."[2] From an allusion to the disastrous English expedition against Portugal in 1589, as well as from the close similarity to the style of Kyd, Dr. Adams more specifically dates it before the extant English versions. He believes it to be based on a truncated text, possibly made for the use of the players when in 1592-4 they were forced by the plague into the provinces. In support of his theory he points out that early in June, 1594, as soon as the plague had subsided, the company that owned the original manuscript returned to London where on the ninth of June as one of its first performances it played *Hamlet*.[3] Obviously a troupe which for purposes of traveling had reduced its numbers to a minimum could hardly reconstruct itself at once into a full city company. Dr. Adams therefore concludes that the truncated version used by the players in the country was probably the one acted on June 9, 1594; also that this manuscript may have been transferred to players who were leaving to tour the Continent, and thus have found its way into Germany.[4]

[1] For detailed accounts of the authorship of the *Ur-Hamlet* see J. Q. Adams, *op. cit.*, pp. 340-1; J. D. Wilson, *Hamlet*, 1934, pp. xvi-xix; E. K. Chambers, *William Shakespeare: A Study of Facts and Problems*, 1930, I, p. 424.

[2] *Op. cit.*, p. xxv.   [3] *Op. cit.*, p. 342.   [4] *Ibid.*, pp. 342-3.

In order to renew the appeal of a successful play, the playwright of the company possessing the manuscript revised it, usually with additions of his own. Sufficient proof of the success of *Hamlet* lies in the evidence already stated, namely, that in abbreviated form it was taken by the players into the provinces; only the most popular dramas were selected for touring purposes. Since the refurbishing of successful old plays usually occurred about every five or six years, it is quite possible that before the end of the century *Hamlet* was subjected to one or two such treatments. And that one revision probably appeared in 1596 may be inferred from the allusion of Thomas Lodge in his *Wit's Miserie* (entered in the Stationers' Registers on May 5, 1596) to a "ghost, which cried so miserably at the Theatre, like an oyster wife, 'Hamlet, revenge!'" Of vast importance to this study is the fact that the playwright for the company possessing the manuscript of *Hamlet* (the Lord Chamberlain's Men, who at the time were playing at the Theatre) was William Shakespeare.[1]

From Lodge's comment it is evident that the scenes which most appealed to the public were those in which the Ghost appeared, and many scholars believe that in these revised ghost scenes Shakespeare may have had a hand. Dr. A. H. Thorndike, who regarded the First Quarto as "Shakespeare's partial revision of the original *Hamlet*," writes:

> So far as Shakespeare had retouched it, he had made it far more poetical, more artistic than its predecessor; he had replaced a ranting ghost with a dignified ghost

[1] *Ibid.*, p. 347.

and had begun to give the reflective passages a phrasing that should make them ever significant.[1]

Dr. Adams suggests that the Poet "probably contented himself with a superficial reworking of the old text—especially the scenes in which the Ghost appeared, and with just enough 'additions' to give the play a fresh appeal." But he adds:

> Although we have many reasons to suppose that such a revamping of the old *Hamlet* was made about 1596, and some cause to suspect Shakespeare's hand in it, definite external evidence is lacking. All we can confidently say is that in 1600 or 1601 the great dramatist undertook a thorough revision of the play.[2]

For the completion of the final version Professor Wilson and Sir. E. K. Chambers also regard 1601 as the latest possible date. Yet they, too, suspect that for several years Shakespeare had been working on it, and indeed that he may have finished his revision long before 1601. Wilson states that some time between June, 1594, and the autumn of 1601 "Shakespeare himself transformed it to the marvel of beauty and subtilty which his fortunate heirs call *Hamlet*."[3] On the basis of Gabriel Harvey's note in Speght's Chaucer,[4] Chambers would recognize Shakespeare's revision at "any date from 1598 to the opening weeks of 1601."[5]

The tragedy soon became so popular that one of the

---

[1] "The Relations of *Hamlet* to Contemporary Revenge Plays," *PMLA*, XVII, (1902), p. 176.

[2] *Op. cit.*, p. 347.

[3] *Op. cit.*, p. xxi.

[4] G. C. Moore Smith, *Gabriel Harvey's Marginalia*, 1913, pp. viii-xii.

[5] *Op. cit.*, II, p. 197.

less important players, from his own actor's part and what he could remember of the parts of others, with the help of an old truncated copy—possibly the one made from the revision of 1596, or even earlier—managed to patch up a defective version and sell it to unscrupulous publishers. This mangled play is known as the First Quarto of *Hamlet* (1603).[1] In order to repair the damage done to his reputation, Shakespeare late in 1604 gave to the press the more correct version, the so-called Second Quarto. Of course, the prompt-book was retained for the use of the actors, and from time to time changes may have been made in this, so that when in 1623 the Folio edition based on that prompt-book came out, it differed somewhat from the earlier authentic quarto, yet not so much as to affect the literature of the period.

A comparison of the finished *Hamlet* with the *Fratricide Punished* and with the First Quarto indicates that Shakespeare is responsible, first of all, for the subtle portrayal of the melancholy Dane, which has evoked so many conflicting interpretations; secondly, for the romantic conception of Ophelia, and therefore the nunnery and mad scenes; thirdly, for the sympathetic treatment of the repentant Queen, who in the final version does not augment her corruption by the betrayal of her second husband, as in the First Quarto; fourthly, for

---

[1] Adams (*op. cit.*, pp. 349-53), Chambers (*op. cit.*, I, p. 415), and Wilson (*op. cit.*, pp. xxv-xxvi) concur in the theory that the First Quarto is a pirated edition. Though Adams and Wilson feel certain that the work of the pirate has been supplemented by the pre-Shakespearean version, Chambers with less conviction writes: "Even if one does not accept Wilson's view as it stands, some contamination of Q1 by the old play is of course a possibility" (*op. cit.*, I, p. 421).

the transformation of the traditional wailing ghost; and finally, for the graveyard scene with its commentary upon the transitoriness of the things of this world. Any imitation of these details by contemporary playwrights will indicate their recognition of Shakespeare's genius. Accordingly, with these definitely Shakespearean features in mind let us apply our touchstone.

II

HAMLET AND CONTEMPORARY TRAGEDIES OF REVENGE

M R. MUNRO'S inconsistency in admitting the overwhelming influence of *Hamlet* while denying that of its author may have come from his unquestioning acceptance of the dictum of Dr. A. H. Thorndike, who seven years before the appearance of the *Allusion-Book* had thus passed upon the very limited collection of allusions previously noted:

> In these allusions, *Hamlet* was looked upon as a popular ghost play, in which the dodging about of the ghost was especially noticeable; as a play to be placed beside old Hieronimo; and as a play whose popularity warranted a little pleasant burlesque. So far as Hamlet's character is touched upon at all, his salient features seem to have been his madness and furious action. The evidence of these few allusions is not very conclusive. They do, however, indicate that *Hamlet* was famous as a play dealing with revenge and a ghost, and they do not hint that it seemed to differ greatly from other revenge-plays. There is no appreciation of its artistic significance.[1]

Thorndike here limits the possible influence of *Hamlet*

[1] *Op. cit.*, p. 203 n. He refers to the allusions in *Shakespeare's Centurie of Prayse* (New Shakespeare Series, IV, 2) and *Fresh Allusions to Shakespeare* (*ibid.*, 3) later incorporated by Munro in his larger collection.

to the tragedy of revenge and to the manner of presenting scenes with ghosts. Yet whatever influence it had as a tragedy of revenge he especially discredits; in fact, he maintains that *Antonio's Revenge* by John Marston had a far greater effect upon the revenge-plays of the day.[1] And Mr. Munro accepts all Thorndike's conclusions with an apology that—

> the dearth of plays of a Shakespearean type is by no means indicative of the superiority in any way of such a man as Marston, who seems to have exercised an influence over the later Revenge tragedy, but is tributive to the subtlety of that art of which no man could win the secret.[2]

Consequently, in our study of the relation of *Hamlet* to the other plays of the day we must first turn to an examination of the tragedies of revenge of the early seventeenth century.

The tragedy of revenge is—to borrow Thorndike's apt definition—"a tragedy whose leading motive is revenge, and whose main action deals with the progress of this revenge, leading to the death of the murderers and often the death of the avenger himself."[3] Its principal agents, then, are the murderer and the avenger. The one is instigated to crime through such motives as ambition or lust; the other is prompted to revenge by a sense of

[1] *Op. cit.*, pp. 200-1: "Shakespeare . . . neither invented the type, for Kyd must be credited with that; nor did he set the fashion from 1599 on, for Marston almost certainly preceded him; nor was he the first to try to invest the old conventions with new imaginative vitality, for Marston's play is surely an ambitious effort to do that."
[2] *Op. cit.*, I, p. xxxiv.
[3] *Op. cit.*, p. 125.

duty, also usually by reminders of the dead; and both are involved in an action of delays or intrigue, of crime and bloodshed, through which the final act of justice is reached. For the purpose of inducing pity and fear, certain stock devices, most of which were popularized by Kyd, came to be regarded as essential: the elaborate display of mourning; the foreshadowing of evil by means of ominous dreams or nosebleeds; the individual overwhelmed by misfortune falling to the ground, and attempting to dig his grave with his dagger; the ghost of the murdered man returning to spur and, of course, to guide the avenger; insanity, real or feigned; and numerous deaths by sensational means.

That Kyd is the father of this dramatic form in English literature is generally accepted, and his *Hieronimo* (c. 1586-87), tremendously popular with the Elizabethan audiences, started a vogue that continued without much change until some time between 1596 and 1600. Then, however, the interest of the playwright apparently shifted from the traditional horrors to the human reactions to them. In short, the plays became, as Thorndike expresses it, more philosophical. His assumption that *Antonio's Revenge* induced this change is based upon two points, namely, date and style: he declares that Marston "almost certainly preceded" Shakespeare and was the first to "invest the old conventions with new imaginative vitality."[1] And until very recently most scholars have accepted Thorndike's conclusions.

In support of the year 1599 as the date of *Antonio and Mellida* and 1599-1600 as that of *Antonio's Revenge*, he refers to the inscriptions on the portraits in the Painter Scene of *Antonio and Mellida*:

[1] See p. 13, note 1.

The "Anno Domini, 1599," and "Aetatis suae 24," (Marston was probably born in 1575) fix the date of the first performance of the first part in 1599. The prologue of the second part indicates that it was acted in the winter, probably, then, the winter of 1599-1600.[1]

Occasional dissenting voices, however, have questioned the authenticity of these dates. Professor J. D. Wilson, for example, writes:

> *Hamlet* is supposed to be indebted to Marston's *Antonio's Revenge*. There are many links between the two plays though the priority of Marston's has not to my thinking been proved.[2]

Stimulated primarily by Dr. Adams' earlier stated conviction that Marston's tragedy was influenced by *Hamlet*,[3] I have elsewhere shown that the playwright's twenty-fourth birthday did not occur until the autumn of 1600; hence that the inscriptions can refer neither to the play nor to its author. Supplementing this somewhat negative criticism, I have suggested 1600 as a more exact date for Marston's first play, and—considering the allusion to "clumzie winter" in the Prologue of *Antonio's Revenge*—1601 for the sequel.[4] It is evident, therefore, that an argument for the precedence of Marston based upon dates alone becomes untenable.

[1] *Op. cit.*, p. 130.
[2] *What Happens in Hamlet*, 1935, p. 55 n.
[3] *A Life of William Shakespeare*, 1925, p. 305.
[4] *PMLA*, LIII (March, 1938), pp. 129-37. In my opinion, the armed Epilogue to *Antonio and Mellida*, which disclaims to be a "peremptory challenger of desert," satirizes the arrogant Epilogue to *Cynthia's Revels* (1600), and thus places Marston's earlier play in 1600. Then, in addition to his admission that he wrote his sequel in the winter, several phrases from it ridiculed by Jonson in his *Poetaster* indicate that *Antonio's Revenge* appeared shortly before Jonson's comedy.

But Dr. Thorndike, assuming the date of *Antonio's Revenge* to be established beyond doubt, advances another argument in Marston's favor. He terms *Antonio's Revenge* "an ambitious effort" to give new life to the tragedy of revenge.[1] A close examination of his discussion reveals that this "effort" resolves itself into two factors, "imaginative style" and "reflective philosophy," or as he later phrases it, "a new tragic diction and a profounder moralizing."[2] That the writer of *Antonio's Revenge* did employ a peculiar style, no one will contradict; that it may be termed imaginative, one might even concede; but that it is new, I question; and that it influenced later writers, I must deny.

As far as I can see, Marston's style in this play is that of the satirists who sought obscurity and roughness in diction. R. M. Alden in his study of the English satire, referring to the "barbarous phraseology of the Marstonian order," expresses the opinion that Marston, though perhaps not the most obscure, was at least the roughest of all the satirists.[3] In the introduction to *The Scourge of Villainy* (1598), wherein Marston outlines the requirements of the formal satire and defends his own peculiar style, his opening phrase indicates his desire to employ a style that will appeal to the discerning reader:

To those that seem *judicial* Perusers.

(III, p. 304)

In the Prologue to *Antonio's Revenge*, echoing these words, he implies that he has deliberately carried over

---

[1] See p. 13, note 1.

[2] *Op. cit.*, pp. 166-7.

[3] *The Rise of Formal Satire in England, under Classical Influence* (*Publications of the University of Pennsylvania*, vol. VII, no. 2, 1899), pp. 129 ff.

his satirical style into his two-part play so that his lines,
heavy both in form and in content, may gain the favor
of the most discriminating critic:

> O that our power
> Could lackey or keep wing with our desires,
> That *with unusèd paize of style and sense,*
> *We might weigh massy in judicious scale.*

> (ll. 27-30)

As we might expect, then, we find the tragedy replete
with such harsh and obscure words and phrases as *sid-
dow, unpaiz'd clutch, beaking, corbèd up, huge plunge,
sinking thought, as to part loath, paize, belk,* and *rifted
jawn.*

Interestingly enough, upon the publication of the satires, and later of the plays, Jonson felt moved to comment. In *Every Man Out of his Humour* (1599), written
about a year after the appearance of the satires, the ridiculous Clove is made to say to his companion Orange:

> Monsieur Orange . . . pr'y thee, let's talke fustian a
> little and gull 'hem: make 'hem beleeve we are great
> schollers.

> (III. iv. 6-8)

Then he launches forth into jargon made up of Marstonian scraps from the satires. Two years later, after the
appearance of *Antonio's Revenge*, Jonson, in the "apolo-
geticall Dialogue" attached to his *Poetaster*, a play directed especially at Marston, wrote:

> But sure I am, three yeeres,
> They did provoke me with their petulant stiles
> On every stage.

> (ll. 83-5)

In the play itself Crispinus, an "ignorant poetaster" (Marston), is forced to disgorge a number of undigested words, several of which appear in *Antonio's Revenge*.[1] Inferring from the similarity of these two parodies that Jonson recognized the identity of style in the satires and the plays, we may conclude that in *Antonio's Revenge* Marston had no intention of introducing a new style into the revenge-play but merely desired to develop the uncouth style that he had previously used in his satires and that in his opinion added dignity to his writings— in other words, the *old satirical*, rather than a "new tragic," diction.

And far from introducing a "profounder moralizing," Marston, like most of his predecessors, packed his work with Senecan tags and numerous borrowings from Montaigne.[2] His "reflective philosophy," therefore, is largely synthetic. Finally, entirely dispelling any notion that he is an innovator, is his tendency to cling to the traditional devices of the revenge-play: the nosebleed significant of impending danger; ominous dreams; the hero in black reading Seneca, or falling to the ground under the weight of his woes; the Ghost delivering a prologue and then withdrawing to observe and comment on the action. No one, of course, would contend that the use of these stock conventions by later playwrights evinces the special influence of Marston but only the strength of a powerful tradition of the past decade. Thus neither the

---

[1] Of the 27 words thus ridiculed by Jonson, 7 appear in *Antonio's Revenge*, 6 in the satires, 5 in *Jack Drum's Entertainment*, 2 in *Antonio and Mellida*; and the remainder come from an unidentified source, perhaps the original version of *What You Will*. See J. Q. Adams, *A Life of William Shakespeare*, p. 323.

[2] *The Plays of John Marston* ed. by H. Harvey Wood, 1934, pp. 224-5.

date hitherto assigned to *Antonio's Revenge* nor the originality ascribed to its author will withstand careful examination.

Yet, though we must take from Marston the distinction of influencing the development of the tragedy of revenge, we may confer on him the honor of being the first to recognize the greatness of *Hamlet*. The resemblance in plot and characterization between *Antonio's Revenge* and the Shakespearean play is unmistakable. When Antonio learns of his father's sudden death and of Mellida's supposed unchastity, he becomes melancholy, and instead of swinging into action broods over his two afflictions:

> My father dead: my love attaint of lust . . .
> What, whom, whither, which shall I first lament?
> *A dead father, a dishonour'd wife?*[1]
> > (I. ii. 264 ff.; cf. *Hamlet*, III. viii. 57)

As he comes upon the stage, dressed in black, book in hand, he tries in vain to explain his state of mind:

> The chamber of my breast is even throng'd
> With firm attendance that forswears to flinch.
> I have a thing sits here; it is not grief,
> 'Tis not despair, nor the [ut]most plague
> That the most wretched are infected with;
> But the most griefful, [most] despairing, wretched,
> Accursèd, miserable.
> > (II. ii. 11-17)

When he visits Mellida in prison and discovers that she has been grossly slandered, he promises to aid her, but like every other victim of melancholia he lacks the necessary energy. All that he can do is "weep, weep" and

[1] *The Plays of John Marston* ed. by A. H. Bullen, 1887.

"sigh" and "wring his hands" and "beat his poor breast" and "wreathe his tender arms." Then no sooner is he satisfied that Mellida is beyond reproach than he learns that his mother is receiving the amorous advances of Piero, who corresponds to the Claudius of Shakespeare's play.[1] Of particular significance in revealing the effect of this last blow is the youth's angry demand:

> Why, mother, is 't not wondrous strange
> I am not mad—I run not frantic, ha?
> Knowing, *my father's trunk scarce cold, your love*
> *Is sought by him that doth pursue my life!*
> (II. ii. 151-4; cf. *Hamlet*, I. ii. 147-51)

In this manner Marston subjects his hero to shocks that quite disillusion him even before the appearance of the Ghost with its dreadful news.

Before Antonio recovers, the Ghost reveals to him not only the foul murder but also the disloyal behavior of his mother, and demands immediate action:

> Antonio, *revenge!*
> I was empoison'd by Piero's hand.
> *Revenge my blood!* take spirit, gentle boy;
> *Revenge my blood* . . .
> Thy mother yields consent
> To be his wife, and give his blood a son,
> That made her husbandless, and doth complot
> To make her sonless.
> (III. i. 34 ff.; cf. *Hamlet*, I. v. 7 ff.)

[1] In the opening lines of *Antonio's Revenge* (I. i. 66-74) Piero discloses that instead of drinking a health to Andrugio (*Antonio and Mellida*, V. i. 365-6) he really dropped "strong poison" into the cup; cf. *Hamlet*, V. ii. 286-7. Like Claudius, he also uses an accomplice, Strotzo, who eventually dies in his own snare; cf. *Hamlet*, V. ii. 311-2.

The young man cries:

> May I be cursèd by my father's ghost,
> And blasted with incensèd breath of Heaven,
> If my heart beat on ought but vengeance!
>
> (III. i. 84-6; cf. *Hamlet*, I. v. 95-7)

Yet he merely dons a "fool's habit," and as an apology for his ridiculous actions he assures his friends that if only he had been born a "good poor fool," he should "want sense to feel" his present anguish. Evidently, like Hamlet's "madness," one purpose of his disguise is to secure emotional relief.[1]

To Antonio, as to Hamlet, comes the critical moment when he can readily punish the villain. As he renews his filial oath, Piero accompanied only by two boys enters. But Antonio hesitates. He "offers to come near and stab," indeed, but "Piero presently withdraws"; and the avenger lamely excuses his inaction with the threat of a more terrible vengeance at some future date.[2] Instead of taking his desired revenge, he murders Piero's innocent son. Thus, like Hamlet, seemingly determined to act, he lets slip his "pat" opportunity with the excuse that he delays in order to make the eventual retribution more severe; and immediately afterward—continuing the parallelism—he kills a person not directly related to the important task of revenge. When a few moments later, drunk with young Julio's blood, he menacingly strides into his mother's room, he meets the Ghost of his father, who restrains him from violence.[3]

---

[1] See *Hamlet* ed. by J. Q. Adams, pp. 228-9.

[2] *Antonio's Revenge*, III. i. 136-9; cf. *Hamlet*, III, ii. 400-2 and III. iii. 73 ff.

[3] Further resemblance to the corresponding scene in *Hamlet* appears in Andrugio's conversation with his wife which parallels Hamlet's conversation with his mother (III. iv):

In still other respects—less important, perhaps, than those already described—the two tragedies show distinct traces of interrelationship. First, the incident in which the Ghost speaks from beneath the stage occurs three times in the same scene in *Antonio's Revenge*: once, as in *Hamlet*, immediately after revealing the treachery of the villain; then a few minutes later when Antonio is on the point of releasing Julio; and again when Julio dies. Secondly, Antonio finds his Horatio in Alberto, whom he takes into his confidence and places under oath to assist in the punishment of Piero. Thirdly, the heroine of *Antonio's Revenge*, falsely informed of the death of her lover, dies offstage of a broken heart; whereupon the mother of the hero rushes in with the account of the sad affair. Finally, the numerous verbal resemblances between the two plays assure us that something more than

---

> Disloyal to our hymeneal rites,
> What raging heat reigns in thy strumpet blood?
> Hast thou so soon forgot Andrugio?
> Are our love-bands so quickly cancellèd?
> Where lives thy plighted faith unto this breast?
> O weak Maria! Go to, calm thy fears.
> I pardon thee, poor soul! O shed no tears;
> Thy sex is weak. That black incarnate fiend
> May trip thy faith that hath o'erthrown my life:
> I was impoison'd by Piero's hand.
> Join with my son to bend up strain'd revenge,
> Maintain a seeming favor to his suit,
> Till time may form our vengeance absolute.
>
> (III. ii. 66-78)

In other words, Andrugio first accuses Maria of infidelity, then warns her of the danger which threatens her soul, and finally urges her to pretend that she knows nothing about the crime. Similarly, Hamlet reproaches his mother for her sin, then advises her to repent, and before he leaves, requests her to conceal everything from the King. In neither instance does the woman disregard the advice.

mere chance has here to be reckoned with.[1] *Antonio's Revenge* contains eighteen fairly obvious echoes of passages in *Hamlet*, whereas its predecessor, *Antonio and Mellida*, has none. Furthermore, each of Marston's subsequent plays has at least one similar allusion. Hence, *Antonio's Revenge* evidently marks the awakening of an interest in Shakespeare's tragedy that Marston retained until the end of his career as a playwright. His constant borrowing in the later plays forces the conclusion that he was imitating Shakespeare in the tragedy of revenge.

In our preoccupation with the similarities between these plays we must not overlook the fact that Marston did not slavishly follow Shakespeare. On the contrary, he seems to be attempting to present a different treatment of revenge. Perhaps, like Mr. H. Harvey Wood, he felt that Shakespeare's play is a "refinement and perversion" of the traditional form.[2] At all events he retains much of the ghastly horror of the revenge-plays of the earlier period. The similarity in circumstances between the murder of Julio and the death of Polonius has been observed,[3] but the fundamental difference has not been mentioned. The murder of Julio, actuated by the Ghost, is horribly deliberate; that of Polonius, accidental. Furthermore, Antonio uses his victim's corpse as the means of increasing Piero's death agonies and thereby adding to his revenge, whereas the killing of Polonius affects Hamlet's vengeance only casually, if at all. Again, the punishment of Claudius may have seemed too mild

---

[1] See pp. 135-8.
[2] *Op. cit.*, p. xxxvi.
[3] See p. 21.

for Marston, for Antonio and his fellow-conspirators bind Piero, pluck out his tongue, and torture him.

Three other tragedies of revenge which appeared at the beginning of the century—*Hoffman, or a Revenge for a Father* (1602), *The Revenge of Bussy d'Ambois* (1604), and *The Atheist's Tragedy, or The Honest Man's Revenge* (1606)—present a similar mixture of imitation and contrast. In Chettle's play the resemblances to *Hamlet* are clear enough. In the opening lines Hoffman, melancholy because of his father's death, bursts forth into self-denunciation for his failure to get revenge. He vows to let nothing stand between him and vengeance, and to the skeleton of his dead parent, which replaces the Ghost as the instigator to action, he exclaims:

> Be but appeas'd, sweete hearse
> The dead remembrance of my living father
> And with a hart as iron, *swift as thought*
> I 'le execute justly in such a cause
> Where truth leadeth.[1]

(ll. 5-9)

Then, confiding in his accomplice, he requests:

> Therefore without protraction, [sighing], or excuses
> *Sweare to be true*, to ayd [assist] me, *not to stirre*
> *Or contradict me in any enterprise*
> *I shall now undertake, or heare after.*[2]

(ll. 71-4)

[1] Cf. HAMLET. Haste me to know 't, that I with *wings as swift*
  As meditation or the thoughts of love
  May sweep to my revenge!

(I. v. 29-31)

[2] Cf. Hamlet's injunction to Horatio and Marcellus after the revelation of the Ghost (I. v. 169-81).

Lucibella and Ophelia have even more in common than the two heroes. The double loss of husband and father affects the mind of Lucibella, who, like the mad Danish girl, comes upon the stage, lamenting her two-fold bereavement:

> For I am going to the rivers side
> To fetch white lillies, and blew daffodils
> To sticke in Lodowicks bosome, where it bled,
> And in mine owne; *my true love is not dead*,
> Noe y 'are deceivd in him, *my father is*.
> > (ll. 1340-4; cf. *Hamlet*, IV. i. 23-40)

When the hermit sympathetically recommends patience, she asks:

> > Pray [ye] tell me true,
> *Could you be patient*, or you, or you, or you,
> *To loose a father and a husband too?*[1]
>
> > (ll. 1355-7)

Her veiled accusations directed toward Hoffman, like the "half sense" of Ophelia, present a "document in madness" to the suspicious bystander:

> I but a knave may kill one by a tricke,
> Or lay a plot, or soe, or cog, or prate,
> Make strife, make a mans father hang him [up],
> Or his brother, how thinke you goodly Prince,
> God give you joy of your adoption;
> May not [such] trickes be usd?
> > (ll. 1377-82; cf. *Hamlet*, IV. i. 4-9)

[1] Cf. Ophelia before the King and Queen, particularly the lines:
I hope all will be well. *We must be patient: but I cannot choose but weep to think they should lay him i' the cold ground.*
> (IV. i. 68-70)

Her kinship with her Shakespearean counterpart she again reveals when she walks off the stage saying:

> O never feare me, there is somewhat cries
> Within me noe: tels me there 's knaves abroad
> Bids mee quiet, lay me downe and sleepe
> *Good night good gentlefolkes,* brother your hand,
> And yours good father, you are my father now . . .
> Soe now god-buye, [*soe*] *now god-night indeede.*[1]
>
> (ll. 1394 ff.)

Among these "unshaped" remarks Lucibella also intersperses snatches of old songs reminiscent of those of Ophelia:

> Here, looke, looke here, here is a way goes downe,
> *Downe, downe a downe, hey downe, downe.*
> I sung that song, while Lodowicke slept with me.[2]
>
> (ll. 1839-41)

We later learn that in her frenzy "like a chased hinde" she "flys through the thickets, and neglects the bryers."[3]

Yet, with the exception of a few other relatively unimportant verbal echoes,[4] the two plays exhibit startling

---

[1] Cf. OPHELIA. I hope all will be well . . . *Good-night, ladies. Good-night, sweet ladies. Good-night! Good-night!*

(IV. i. 68 ff.)

[2] Cf. OPHELIA. You must sing, "*A-down a-down!*" and you, "*Call him a-down-a!*" O how the wheel becomes it! It is the false steward that stole his master's daughter.

(IV. i. 169-71)

[3] ll. 1537-8; cf. *Hamlet*, IV. iii. 165-74.

[4] See pp. 140-1. Perhaps we should also include the remark of the "witlesse foole" Jerom—

True, I am no foole, I have bin *at Wittenberg*, where wit growes.

(ll. 260-1)

differences. Chettle may have felt that Ophelia's insanity, which serves chiefly to increase the tragic effect, has too little to do with the action, for in his play Lucibella's madness enables her to spy upon Hoffman and deliver him at last to justice. The behavior of Chettle's heroine is so purposeful that at times we cannot help wondering if she really is mad; consequently her actions fail to produce that effect of pity evoked by the helpless Ophelia. In addition, the hero's vindictiveness seems almost maniacal; Hoffman, indeed, plays a double rôle of hero and villain. By no means a "noble youth . . . most generous and free from all contriving," who needs a Ghost from the tomb to goad him into action, he with utmost dispatch punishes the main agent of his father's death and, with only a skeleton as his "cue," proceeds to annihilate all the relatives and friends of his victim. Thus Chettle portrays the son of a murdered father, who through his own efforts achieved a most horrible vengeance and would have laughed irresolution to scorn.

An entirely different aspect of the revenge-motif presents itself in *The Revenge of Bussy d'Ambois*, in which the hero Clermont finds it his duty to punish the murderer of his brother; yet here again appear unmistakable resemblances to Shakespeare's play. Like Hamlet, the avenger, both scholar and soldier,[1] is far too noble to

[1] GUISE.   That Clermont is my love;
France never bred *a nobler gentleman*
For all parts . . .
                    Besides his valour,
He hath the crown of man, and all his parts,
Which learning is; and that so true and virtuous
That it gives power to do as well as say
Whatever fits a most accomplished man.
                    (II. i. 80 ff.; cf. *Hamlet*, III. i. 156)

suspect deceit in his fellowmen, and when he falls into
the hands of his enemies, the Countess of Cambrai comments:

> They could not all have taken Clermont d'Ambois
> Without their treachery; he had bought his bands out
> With their slave bloods; but he was credulous;
> He would believe, since he would be believ'd;
> Your noblest natures are most credulous.[1]

(IV. iii. 77-81)

But Clermont, unlike Hamlet, no sooner ascertains the
identity of his brother's murderer than he challenges the
guilty man to a duel. At the craven Montsurrey's refusal
to fight, the "Senecal man," not at all disconcerted,
calmly bides his time; all his friends are far more perturbed than he. On one occasion, angered by his metic-
ulous defense of his forbearance, his sister, who misinter-
prets stoical calm for cowardice, cries:

> Dispute, when you should fight! Wrong, wreakless
>   sleeping,
> Makes men die honourless; one borne, another
> Leaps on our shoulders.

He impassively replies:

> We must wreak our wrongs
> So we take not more.

(III. ii. 103-4)

Even his brother's Ghost cannot disturb his serenity.
In a scene clearly reminiscent of the apparition in Gertrude's chamber, the indignant spirit rises to the stage:

---

[1] Hamlet likewise is caught by treachery because he is "remiss, most
generous, and free from all contriving" (IV. iii. 133-4).

> Once more I ascend,
> And bide the cold damp of this piercing air,
> To urge the justice whose almighty word
> Measures the bloody acts of impious men
> With equal penance.
>
> (V. i. 3-7)

And visible only to Clermont it demands prompt action:

> Danger (the spur of all great minds) is ever
> The curb to your tame spirits . . .
> *Away, then! Use the means thou hast to right*
> *The wrong I suffer'd.*
>
> (V. i. 78 ff.; cf. *Hamlet*, III. iv. 106-10)

As the avenger stands dazed, his companion inquires:

> Why stand'st thou still thus, and *apply'st thine ears*
> *And eyes to nothing?*

Echoing Hamlet's astounded response to his mother, Clermont asks:

> *Saw you nothing there?*

His friend reassures him:

> *Thou dream'st awake now; what was here to see?*

Clermont then explains his amazement:

> *My brother's spirit urging his revenge.*[1]
>
> (V. i. 100-3)

[1] QUEEN.   Alas, how is 't with you,
>   *That you do bend your eye on vacancy . . .*
> HAMLET.   *Do you see nothing there?*
> QUEEN. *Nothing at all; yet all that is I see . . .*
> HAMLET. Why look you! there! Look, how it steals away!
>   *My father, in his habit as he liv'd!*
>
> (III. iv. 115 ff.)

Yet, in spite of the censure of his companions, the reproach of his family, and even the entreaty of a brother's spirit, he delays, not like his predecessor because of melancholia, but rather on account of his stout determination to meet Montsurrey in fair fight. The very fact that Chapman imitates the ghost scene in *Hamlet* only accentuates the difference in his attitude toward revenge, for the appearance of the Ghost, which in the Shakespearean play so powerfully affects the hero, does not in the least alter Clermont's resolution to wait until he can meet Montsurrey face to face and force him to a duel. Chapman's hero therefore stands above reproach even in revenge, in which much latitude was permitted. Through Clermont's rational approach to his problem the playwright questions Hamlet's emotional instability, his postponement of revenge despite frequent opportunity, and finally his method of punishing the murderer.[1]

But the most pointed reply to Shakespeare's *Hamlet* is Tourneur's *Atheist's Tragedy*, which in scene after scene and line after line echoes the earlier play and yet at the same time betrays the critical attitude of the author toward that play.[2] D'Amville, the villainous uncle, persuades his nephew Charlemont to go to war contrary to his father's wish. The young man, it must be admitted, needs little urging, for his high spirit welcomes action. Castabella, his betrothed, well describes his nobility of soul when she defends his departure:

[1] See also T. M. Parrott, *The Tragedies of George Chapman*, 1910, p. 573.

[2] See J. Q. Adams, *A Life of William Shakespeare*, pp. 305-6.

> 'Tis a *generous mind*
> That led his disposition to the war:
> For *gentle love* and *noble courage* are
> So near allied, that one begets another;
> Or Love is sister and Courage is the brother.
> Could I affect him better than before,
> His *soldier's* heart would make me love him more.
> (I. iv. pp. 260-1; cf. *Hamlet*, III. i. 155-6)

As soon as the son is safely out of the way, D'Amville murders the father and seizes his possessions; whereupon, in a dream, the Ghost of the murdered man bids his son:

> Return to France, for thy old father's dead,
> And thou by murder disinherited.
> (II. vi. p. 286)

Charlemont's startled exclamation, "O my affrighted soul!" recalls Hamlet's "O my prophetic soul!" upon learning of his uncle's crime. Since Charlemont doubts the authenticity of the Ghost's information, the Ghost immediately reappears both to him and to the soldier on guard, who Marcellus-like challenges it:

> *Stand! Stand, I say!* No? Why then have at thee,
> Sir. *If you will not stand*, I'll make you fall. [*Fires.*
> Nor stand nor fall? Nay then, the devil's dam
> Has broke her husband's head, for sure *it is*
> *A spirit.*
> *I shot it through, and yet it will not fall.*
> (II. vi. p. 287; cf. *Hamlet*, I. i. 139-46)

When Charlemont returns home, he finds that he has been not only "disinherited" but also dispossessed of Castabella. Like Hamlet, he at once recognizes his uncle's treachery, and he now understands why the villain urged him to go to war:

> A close advantage of my absence made
> To dispossess me both of land and wife,
> And all the profit does arise to him
> By whom my absence was first moved and urged.
> *These circumstances, uncle, tell me you*
> *Are the suspected author of those wrongs,*
> *Whereof the lightest is more heavy than*
> *The strongest patience can endure to bear.*[1]

(III. i. p. 293)

His concluding words indicate an utter disillusionment, that at once plunges him into a state of melancholia. When his uncle suspiciously tries to sound him—

> Your sadness and the sickness of my son
> Have made our company and conference
> Less free and pleasing than I purposed it—

Charlemont, desirous of solitude, rebuffs him:

> Sir, for the present I am much unfit
> For conversation or society.
> With pardon I will rudely take my leave.[2]

D'Amville then tells his accomplice that—

> Sad melancholy has drawn Charlemont
> With meditation on his father's death
> Into the solitary walk behind the church.

(IV. ii. p. 305-6)

---

[1] Cf. HAMLET.   O my prophetic soul!
>   *My uncle?* . . .
>   The time is out of joint; O cursed spite
>   That ever I was born to set it right.

(I. v. 40 ff.)

[2] See Dr. Adams' discussion of this symptom of melancholia in his edition of *Hamlet*, p. 196.

This remark heralds an imitation of the graveyard scene. A few moments later we find Charlemont in the churchyard meditating upon the vanity of life:

> This grave—Perhaps the inhabitant was in his lifetime
> the possessor of his own desires. Yet in the midst of
> all his greatness and his wealth he was less rich and
> less contented than in this poor piece of earth lower
> and lesser than a cottage. For here he neither wants
> nor cares. Now that his body savours of corruption
> He enjoys a sweeter rest than e'er he did
> Amongst the sweetest pleasures of this life,
> For here there's nothing troubles him.—And there
> —In that grave lies another. He, perhaps,
> Was in his life as full of misery
> As this of happiness. And here's an end
> Of both. Now both their states are equal. O
> That man with so much labour should aspire
> To worldly height, when in the humble earth
> The world's condition's at the best, or scorn
> Inferior men, since to be lower than
> A worm is to be higher than a king.
>
> (IV. iii. pp. 307-8; cf. *Hamlet*, V. i. 101 ff.)

It seems unnecessary now to state that D'Amville is patterned upon the usurping King of Denmark. Almost paraphrasing Claudius' honeyed admonitions to Hamlet, the Atheist expresses insincere sympathy and feigned paternal affection for his nephew:

> *To lose a father and*, as you may think,
> *Be disinherited*, it must be granted
> *Are motives to impatience. But for death*,
> *Who can avoid it?* And for his estate,
> In the uncertainty of both your lives
> 'Twas done discreetly to confer't upon

A known successor being the next in blood.
And one, dear nephew, whom in time to come
You shall have cause to thank. *I will not be*
Your dispossessor but your guardian.
I will supply your father's vacant place
To guide your green improvidence of youth,
And make you ripe for your inheritance.[1]

(III. iv. p. 300)

Just as Claudius is suspected, erroneously indeed, of having evil designs upon Ophelia,[2] so—Tourneur expanding this suggestion—D'Amville actually does attempt to seduce Castabella, his son's wife formerly betrothed to Charlemont. Upon occasions, too, the murderer becomes conscience-stricken:

> But now that I begin to feel the loathsome horror of my sin, and, like a lecher emptied of his lust, desire to bury my face under my eye-brows, and would steal from my shame unseen, she meets me

---

[1] Cf. KING. 'Tis sweet and commendable in your nature, Hamlet,
　　　　To give these mourning duties to your father.
　　　　But, you must know, *your father lost a father;*
　　　　That father lost, lost his; and the survivor bound
　　　　In filial obligation for some term
　　　　To do obsequious sorrow: but to persever
　　　　In obstinate condolement is a course.
　　　　Of impious stubbornness . . .
　　　　　　　　　　We pray you, throw to earth
　　　　This unprevailing woe; *and think of us*
　　　　As of a father. For—let the world take note!—
　　　　You are the most immediate to our throne;
　　　　And with no less nobility of love
　　　　Than that which dearest father bears his son
　　　　Do I impart toward you.

(I. ii. 87 ff.)

[2] See J. Q. Adams, *Hamlet*, pp. 237-9.

I' the face with all her light corrupted eyes
To challenge payment o' me . . .

              Why, was I born a coward?
He lies that says so. Yet the countenance of
A bloodless worm might ha' the courage now
To turn my blood to water.
The trembling motion of an aspen leaf
Would make me, like the shadow of that leaf,
Lie shaking under 't. *I could now commit*
A murder were it but to drink the fresh
Warm blood of him I murdered to supply
The want and weakness o' mine own,
'Tis grown so cold and phlegmatic.[1]

        (IV. iii. p. 315; cf. *Hamlet*, III. iii. 36 ff.)

Thus, in every detail—usurper, flatterer, incestuous seducer, and murderer—the villain of *The Atheist's*
Tragedy follows the villain of *Hamlet*.

Nevertheless, Tourneur has constructed a theory of
revenge directly opposed to Shakespeare's. We have already discussed the similarity between the initial visit of
the Ghost in *The Atheist's Tragedy* and the appear-

---

[1] Note also the verbal resemblance to Hamlet's soliloquies:
              Am I a coward?
Who calls me villain? breaks my pate across?
Plucks off my beard and blows it in my face?
Tweaks me by the nose? gives me the lie i' the throat
As deep as to the lungs? . . .
Swounds, I should take it; for it cannot be
But I am pigeon-liver'd and lack gall
To make oppression bitter . . .
                  (II. ii. 586-94)
           Now could I drink hot blood!
And do such bitter business as the day
Would quake to look on!
                  (III. ii. 400-2)

ance of the Ghost of the Danish King to Horatio and Marcellus.[1] Later, just as the Ghost of the elder Hamlet interferes in order to check his son's wrath toward Gertrude, innocent at least of murder, so Montferrer's Ghost prevents Charlemont from injuring D'Amville's guiltless son. Although on both occasions Tourneur's Ghost in the circumstances of its appearance resembles that of Shakespeare, it comes with an entirely different purpose. The first time it warns the hero to—

> Attend with patience the success of things,
> But leave revenge unto the King of kings.
>
> (II. vi. p. 286)

And the second time it exclaims:

> Hold, Charlemont!
> Let him revenge my murder and thy wrongs
> To whom the justice of revenge belongs.
>
> (III. ii. p. 294)

Thus Charlemont's inaction is justified by his father's Ghost, whereas Hamlet regards his father's message as the very "cue" for action.

In the failure of D'Amville's schemes and in his terrible death Tourneur demonstrates the workings of divine justice and hence the futility of revenge. After the Atheist has committed frightful crimes in order to accumulate a fortune for his two sons, he finds them utterly unfit to inherit it—the elder impotent and the younger dissolute, both of whom die even before his own downfall. Then, as he is about to execute the hero, he dashes out his own brains instead. Fortunately he

[1] See p. 31.

lives long enough to confess his crimes and thereby ab-
solve his intended victim, who for the edification of the
audience exclaims:

> Only to Heaven I attribute the work,
> Whose gracious motives made me still forbear
> To be mine own revenger. Now I see
> That patience is the honest man's revenge.[1]
>
> (V. ii. p. 336)

It is evident, therefore, that contemporary playwrights
regarded *Hamlet* as at least a challenge, whereas they
completely ignored *Antonio's Revenge*. Indeed, when
they wanted to typify the avenger, they chose Hamlet,
not Antonio or another. Thus in *Satiromastix* (Thomas
Dekker, 1602) we find the exclamation "My name's
Hamlet revenge!" (I, p. 229), and similarly in *Westward
Hoe* (Thomas Dekker, 1604) "Let these husbands play

---

[1] In *The Revenger's Tragedy* (1607), generally ascribed to Tourneur, we find set forth, though by no means so completely, the same
theory of divine justice. When Lusurioso lies about his seduction of
Castiza in order to persuade her brother Vendice to kill Piato (Vendice in disguise), Vendice cries:

> Has not Heaven an ear? is all the lightning wasted?
>
> (IV. ii. p. 409)

Then a few moments later:

> O thou almighty patience! 'tis my wonder
> That such a fellow, impudent and wicked,
> Should not be cloven as he stood;
> Or with a secret wind burst open!
> Is there no thunder left: or is 't kept up
> In stock for heavier vengeance?
>
> (IV. ii. p. 411)

In both passages the playwright implies that to God alone belongs
vengeance. At the end of the play the two avengers are publicly de-
nounced as common criminals and put to death.

mad Hamlet, and cry revenge" (II, p. 353). Hence, not only imitations, but direct references, few though these may be, support the theory that *Hamlet* revived the notable interest in the tragedy of revenge at the beginning of the seventeenth century. With this evidence before us, the question of the priority of Marston's play ceases to be of moment.

THREE LATER REVENGE-PLAYS

BEFORE turning to the later revenge-plays, let us pause a moment to consider Shakespeare's adaptation of the traditions of Kyd and his imitators. The great Poet with his understanding of dramatic technique would scarcely discard anything that might contribute to the tragic effect. Accordingly, the Ghost appears crying for revenge true to accepted tradition. Hamlet experiences the same sense of filial obligation that weighed upon his predecessors; his ironical remarks and his elaborate display of mourning, as well as his feigned madness, follow the established convention. The King's employment of Polonius and of Rosencrantz and Guildenstern in order to ascertain the reason for the Prince's strange behavior adds to the plot the usual element of intrigue. As for bloodshed, Horatio's summary (V. ii. 385-90) is sufficient proof that the play had its share. Yet in Shakespeare's hands all these old conventions are transformed, and each is so incorporated with the plot that it loses any mechanical quality. Everything else that might render the play ridiculous or unreal, he discards. At the same time he adds several entirely new touches to the old theme: the tragedy of the human soul, exemplified by the disillusionment of the idealistic hero; the broken romance; and the Christianized Ghost. In short, he was the first to see the opportunities for dealing with charac-

ter, and his finished product was so effective that his
successors had to follow in his footsteps. Their recognition of his ability merely as a writer of the revenge-play
will be obvious in an examination of three tragedies of
revenge of a somewhat later date than those already discussed—*The Unnatural Combat* (Philip Massinger,
1626), *The Fatal Contract* (William Heminge, 1630),
and *Aglaura* (John Suckling, 1637).

The Unnatural Combat, which treats of revenge for
a mother, contains the usual resemblances to *Hamlet*.
Like Claudius, Malefort Senior is guilty of adultery, in-
cest, and murder. He is described as seemingly valiant—

> But with that, *bloody; liberal in his gifts* too,
> But to maintain his prodigal expense,
> A fierce extortioner; *an impotent lover*
> *Of women.*
>
> (I, pp. 172-3; cf. *Hamlet*, I. v. 42 ff.)

He has arranged for a second marriage during the life
of his first wife, whom later he poisons. The exact details of this crime are not given, but the stage direction—

> Enter the Ghost of young Malefort . . . leading in the
> Shadow of a Lady, *her face leprous—*
>
> (I, p. 227; cf. *Hamlet*, I. v. 64-73)

suggests that the poison has caused her skin to break out
in a "most lazar-like tetter." In addition, the villain is
overcome with an incestuous love for his own daughter.
His enraged conscience eventually causes him to suffer
untold agonies, and on one occasion when he sees the
ghosts of his victims, he admits his guilt and cries out in
agony:

Can any penance expiate my guilt,
Or can repentance save me?[1]

(I, p. 228)

But his will, like that of the Danish usurper, is so perverted that salvation for him is impossible.

Malefort Junior knows that his mother has been murdered by his father, and because he feels bound to avenge her death but dreads to act, he becomes melancholy. His friends thus describe him:

Sigh he did often, as if inward grief
And melancholy at that instant would
Choke up his vital spirits, and now and then
A tear or two, as in derision of
The roughness of his rugged temper, would
Fall on his hollow cheeks.

(I, p. 147)

He, too, realizes that he must "hold his tongue":

                    May the cause,
That forces me to this unnatural act
Be buried in everlasting silence,
And I find rest in death, or my revenge!
To either I stand equal.[2]

(I, p. 148)

Yet, anxious to keep his good name unsullied, he desires his comrades to understand that neither madness nor

[1] Cf. KING.   What then? What rests?
        Try what repentance can? What can it not?
        Yet *what can it, when one can not repent!*
                                    (*Hamlet*, III. iii. 64-6)

[2] Cf. *Hamlet*, I. ii. 159; also—
HAMLET. *The rest is silence.*

(V. ii. 363)

fear of death causes his hesitation and consequent mental anguish:

> Pray you, gentlemen,
> Be charitable in your censures of me,
> And do not entertain the false belief
> That I am mad, for undertaking that
> Which must be, when effected, still repented.
> It adds to my calamity, *that I have*
> *Discourse and reason,* and but too well know
> I can nor live, nor end a wretched life,
> But both ways I am impious. Do not, therefore,
> Ascribe the perturbation of my soul
> To a servile fear of death: I oft have view'd
> All kinds of his inevitable darts,
> Nor are they terrible. Were I condemn'd to leap
> From the cloud-cover'd brows of a steep rock,
> Into the deep; or, Curtius like, to fill up,
> For my country's safety, and an after-name,
> A bottomless abyss, or charge through fire,
> It could not so much shake me, as th 'encounter
> Of this day's single enemy.[1]

(I, pp. 148-9)

Finally he fights a duel with his father, who kills him; and, like Hamlet, he is given a "soldier's funeral."[2] Unlike the avenger of the typical revenge-play, Malefort

---

[1] Cf. *Hamlet*, I. ii. 131-2; I. v. 189-90; V. ii. 349-50. Note also the verbal echo—

> HAMLET. Sure He that made us with such large *discourse*,
>   Looking before and after, gave us not
>   That capability and god-like *reason*
>   To fust in us unus'd.

(III. viii. 36-9)

[2] I, p. 157; cf. *Hamlet*, V. ii. 401.

Junior dies without accomplishing his revenge, and the villain thus is left to be destroyed by divine wrath.

Frequently in one of these later plays we find several characters who on different occasions will recall the same person in the Shakespearean play. In *The Fatal Contract*, the most obvious and detailed example of plagiarism of *Hamlet* in the seventeenth century,[1] both Clovis and Clotair, the two Princes in love with Aphelia, resemble the Prince of Denmark. Occasionally, too, an individual in these later plays may combine in his nature the qualities of two or more characters in *Hamlet*. The Queen, the arch-villain, possesses all that is bad in both Claudius and Gertrude; she is modelled, indeed, upon the Danish Queen, but is far more positively evil.

As the play begins, she is plotting to murder the King, who is aware of her adulterous love for her favorite Landrey, but who fears to punish her because she is—

> great in faction,
> *Followed and sainted by the multitude,*
> *Whose judgement* she hath linck'd unto her Purse.[2]
>
> (I. i. sig. B2ʳ)

Incidentally, she also desires to avenge the death of her brother. In order to accomplish both purposes at once, she arranges a masque, to which she invites Lamot and Dumaine, the sons of her brother's murderers; in the meantime she poisons her husband so that when he suc-

---

[1] First pointed out by Joseph Q. Adams, "William Heminge and Shakespeare," in *Modern Philology*, XII, (1914), pp. 51-64.

[2] Cf. KING. Yet must not we put the strong law on him:
   He's lov'd of the distracted multitude,
   Who like not in their judgment, but their eyes.
   (*Hamlet*, III. vii. 3-5)

cumbs during the masque she can attribute his death to
her two enemies whom she has had placed near him. At
first Prince Clovis learns only of his mother's shameful
passion, but when, disguised in his dead father's garments, he demands the name of her paramour, she, thinking him a ghost, in terror confesses the murder as well.
This disclosure clearly parallels that in *Hamlet* when the
hero, aware only of his mother's incestuous marriage,
learns from the Ghost the details of the murder. The ensuing scene in *The Fatal Contract* quite appropriately is
modelled upon Hamlet's interview with his mother. To
Clovis' horrified denunciation—

> O that I had no eyes, so you no shame;
> *Murther your Husband* to arrive at lust,
> And then to lay the blame on innocents?
> *Blush, blush, thou worse than woman—*

the Queen replies:

> How dar'st thou cloth thy speech in such a phrase
> To me *thy naturall mother?*

But he is deaf to any appeal to filial duty:

> My mother!
> Adulterate woman, *shame of Royaltie*
> *I blush to call thee mother;* thy foul lusts
> Have taught me words of that harsh consequence
> That Stigmatize obedience, *and do brand*
> *With mis-becoming accents filiall duty.*[1]
>
> (IV. iii. sig. H^v)

[1] QUEEN. Have you forgot me?
 HAMLET.   No, by the rood, not so,
   You are *"the Queen,"* your husband's brother's wife,
   And—*would it were not so!—you are my mother! . . .*
 QUEEN. What have I done, *that thou dar'st wag thy tongue*
   In noise so rude against me?

She is so evil, however, that he fails to move her to repentance.

Aphelia, the heroine, resembles Ophelia in character as well as in name; her companions call her the "fair Aphelia," the "chaste and beautiful" Aphelia. She is the daughter of old Brissac, the King's counsellor, who, like Polonius, is oversolicitous for his daughter's virtue. When her brother Charles brings Prince Clovis to visit her, the old man immediately suspects evil:

> Plots, plots, meer fetches to delude me.
> > (II. i. sig. C3ᵛ; cf. *Hamlet*, I. iii. 115)

Apparently he has already warned Aphelia, for in her first meeting with the Prince she spurns his advances. Like the daughter of old Polonius, she does not "know what she should think." In fact, hearing the reproaches of her lover, she likewise is forced to admit:

> I am too fond, *and yet he swears he loves me,*
> I have believ'd him too, for I have found
> A Godlike nature in him, and a truth
> Hitherto constant.[1]
> > (I. iii. sig. Cᵛ)

HAMLET.   Such an act
> *That blurs the grace and blush of modesty!*
> Calls virtue hypocrite! takes off the rose
> From the fair forehead of an innocent love
> *And sets a blister there!*
> > (III. iv. 14 ff.)

[1] Cf. OPHELIA. He hath importun'd me with love
> In honourable fashion . . .
> And hath given countenance to his speech, my lord,
> *With almost all the holy vows of heaven.*
> > (I. iii. 110 ff.)

Aloud to him she explains:

> If this should be dissembled, not your heart,
> And having won my souls affection,
> *Should on a judgement more retir'd to state*
> *Smile at your perjuries, and leave me in love;*
> What ill-bred tales the world would make of me?
>
> (I. iii. sig. C^v; cf. *Hamlet*, I. iii. 14-21)

As soon as old Brissac satisfies himself that the Prince really loves his daughter, like the Lord High Chamberlain of Denmark he recognizes his tactical blunder:

> *He is in love that's certain;* let me remember,
> *When I was first a lover as he is,*
> *I'd just such wild vagaries in my brain,*
> *Such midnight madness;* this puling baggage
> May lose her self for ever, and her fortunes,
> By this hours absence.[1]
>
> (II. i. sig. C4^r-C4^v)

Aphelia also brings disillusionment to her lover when she leaves him—forced indeed—for his brother Clotair.

Besides the fact that Prince Clotair possesses a "nature mild and gentle" (IV. i. sig. G2^r) his first meeting with Aphelia indicates that Heminge again has Hamlet in his

---

[1] Cf. POLONIUS. *This is the very ecstasy of love,*
    Whose violent property fordoes itself
    And leads the will to desperate undertakings
    As oft as any passion under heaven
    That does afflict our natures. I am sorry . . .
    I am sorry that with better heed and judgment
    I had not quoted him.

    (II. i. 102 ff.)

POLONIUS. He is far gone! far gone! And, truly, *in my youth I suffered much extremity for love.*

    (II. ii. 189-91)

mind's eye. Entering from the rear of the stage, the Prince sees the girl looking at a book containing "words pure," given her to read while she waits, and he comments upon her beauty:

> She ha's a ravishing feature, and her mind
> Is of a purer temper than her body.
> (II. ii. sig. D^r; cf. Hamlet, III. i. 89-90)

Again like the Danish Prince, before he dies he nominates his successor, and, apprehensive for his reputation, anxiously begs his friends:

> Good gentle souls when ye shal mention me,
> And elder time shall rip these stories up,
> Dissected and Anatomiz'd by you;
> Touch sparingly this story, do not read
> Too harsh a comment on this loathed deed,
> Lest you inforce posterity to blast
> My name and Memory with endlesse curses.
> (V. ii. sig. K2^v; cf. Hamlet, V. ii. 343 ff.)

Among minor imitations we may place Charles Brissac, the Counsellor's son and Aphelia's brother, who, like Laertes, leads the rebels to avenge his father's death. Prince Clovis, one of the "Hamlets" of the play, describes him as—

> A hopeful *youth*, *fraught with Nobility*,
> And all the graceful qualities that write
> Man truly honourable.[1]

(IV. iii. sig. H2^r)

[1] Cf. HAMLET.
   A very noble youth.

That is Laertes—

(V. i. 233-4)

It also may be that Heminge had Horatio in mind when he informs us that the two soldiers Lamot and Dumaine have been in Wittenberg.[1] These imitations of character and scene are reënforced by countless verbal echoes; for example, among the welter of borrowings from the three ghost scenes Hamlet's exclamation, "O my prophetic soul," appears three times and his "Hold, hold, my heart," no less than four times.[2]

In *Aglaura*, as in Heminge's play, we find numerous examples of multiple imitation. Zorannes, the son of a murdered father, and the Prince, hated by an ambitious uncle, both remind us of Hamlet. Then again, the King, who has killed Zorannes' father and stolen his betrothed, suggests Claudius; similarly, Ariaspes, plotting to kill his brother the King, resembles the Danish villain. Zorannes' revenge for his father is, of course, an important subplot of this play. "Three tedious winters" the youth has lingered in disguise about Court, hoping that eventually he may punish the King, who has wronged him much as Claudius injures Hamlet—

> *The hopes of all my youth,*
> And a reward which Heav'n hath settled on me
> (If holy contracts can do anything)
> *He ravish'd from me, kill'd my father—*
> Aglaura's father, sir—*would have whor'd my sister,*
> And murthered my friend.[3]
>
> (V. iv. 80-5 as presented at Court)

[1] I. i. sig. B3ʳ; cf. *Hamlet*, I. ii. 164.
[2] See pp. 200-3. For full details see Adams, *op. cit.*
[3] Cf. HAMLET. *He that hath kill'd my king, and whor'd* my mother,
> *Popp'd in between the election and my hopes,*
> Thrown out his angle for my proper life,
> And with such cozenage.
>
> (V. ii. 64-7)

During this interval his father's Ghost has haunted him incessantly, and when at last he decides to act, he exclaims with relief:

> Down, sorrow, down,
> And swell my heart no more! *and thou, wrong'd ghost*
> *Of my dead father, to thy bed again,*
> *And sleep securely!*[1]

> (I. ii. 25-8)

His distress is aggravated by the infidelity of Orbella, once his mistress but now the Queen, whom he has found false not only to him but even to her husband. In his comment to his sister weeping over her dead lover, he sums up his utter disillusionment in women:

> Fie! those tears
> A bride upon the marriage-day as properly
> Might shed as thou:
> Here widows do 't, and marry next day after.
> (V. ii. 79-82; cf. *Hamlet*, III. ii. 128-30)

Naturally his misfortunes have tinged with a melancholy cast his whole outlook upon life. We may assume from his discourse upon the immorality of suicide that the thought of self-slaughter was by no means new to his mind:

> For ever? Ay, there 's it!
> For in those groves thou talk'st of,
> There are so many byways and odd turnings,
> Leading unto such wide and dismal places,
> That should we go without a guide, or stir
> Before heav'n calls, 'tis strongly to be feared,

[1] Cf. HAMLET. *Rest, rest, perturbed spirit!*

> (I. v. 183)

We there should wander up and down for ever,
And be benighted to eternity.[1]

(V. ii. 56-63)

And his reply to Orbella's question regarding the King's
health proves beyond doubt his utter weariness of life:

If to be free from *the great load we sweat*
And labour under here on earth, be to
Be well, he is.[2]

(V. iii. 28-30)

The King's brother, Ariaspes, is filled with criminal
ambition for the throne, but in accomplishing his wicked

[1] Note the similarity in thought and rhythm to Hamlet's meditation
on the same subject:

To sleep? perchance to dream! Ay, there's the rub!
For in that sleep of death what dreams may come,
When we have shuffled off this mortal coil,
Must give us pause . . .
But that the dread of something after death,
That undiscover'd country, from whose bourn
No traveller returns, puzzles the will,
And makes us rather bear those ills we have
Than fly to others that we know not of.

(III. i. 65 ff.)

[2] Suckling wrote two concluding acts to this play—the first, tragic,
for the city, and the second, tragi-comic, for the Court, Zorannes'
reply, quoted above, is changed in the second version to—

If to be on's *journey to the other world*
Be to be well, he is.

(V. iii. 16-7)

Thus, for both versions Suckling goes to the same soliloquy in *Hamlet*:

Who would *fardels bear*,
To grunt and sweat under a weary life,
But that the dread of something after death,
The undiscover'd country, from whose bourn
No traveller returns, puzzles the will.

(III. i. 76-80)

ends he is forced to move cautiously because "the people love the prince."[1] In the tragic version, intending to dispose of the Prince, he is represented as tricked by Zorannes into killing the King instead; then he himself dies upon the avenger's sword. Further increasing his resemblance to Claudius is his incestuous love for the Queen. Despite the fact that she formerly was Zorannes' mistress, her infatuation for her brother-in-law clearly identifies her with Gertrude. This resemblance to Gertrude appears even more clearly in the scene where Zorannes, like Hamlet in his determination to show his mother "more truly how she looks," enters Orbella's room and informs her of the death of her husband and of her lover Ariaspes. When he throws her paramour's corpse down before her, she realizes her own danger and cries:

> Why? thou wilt not murder me too,
> Wilt thou, villain?

He answers:

> I do not know my temper.

Then casting off his disguise, he accuses her of infidelity:

> Look here, vain thing, and see thy sins full blown:
> There's scarce a part in all this face thou hast
> Not been forsworn by, and Heav'n forgive thee for 't!
> For thee I lost a father, country, friends,
> Myself almost.
>   (V. iii. 90-6; cf. *Hamlet*, III. iv. 19-22)

Even if one were to ignore all parallelism in scene and

[1] IV. iii. 78; cf. *Hamlet*, IV. iii. 16-24.

in characters in these later revenge-plays, the numerous verbal echoes alone would suffice to indicate that *Hamlet* was foremost in the minds of playwrights. And a direct reference in Randolph's *Hey For Honesty, Down With Knavery* (1629)—

> By Jeronymo, her looks are as terrible as Don Andrea or *the Ghost in Hamlet*—
>
> (II, p. 414)

gives further evidence of the enduring impression left by *Hamlet*. Randolph evidently regarded *The Spanish Tragedy* and Shakespeare's play as the chief examples of the revenge-play, but *Hamlet* alone is imitated on the stage. Recalling the critical, questioning attitude of playwrights at the beginning of the century toward the Shakespearean treatment of the revenge-motif, we now observe that *Hamlet* ultimately emerges as the sole model for the tragedy of revenge.

IV

HAMLET AND BEAUMONT AND FLETCHER

M UNRO, it will be recalled, states that Beaumont
and Fletcher rather than Shakespeare influenced
the drama of the period, and he warns us not to expect
to find any plays on a Shakespearean model before the
year 1660.[1] How surprising it is, then, to find Beaumont
and Fletcher themselves borrowing from *Hamlet* not
only for their relatively unimportant venture into the
tragedy of revenge, *Four Plays or Moral Representations
in One* (1608), but even for two of their greatest works,
Philaster, or Love lies a Bleeding (1610) and *The Maids
Tragedy* (1611). Incidentally, the evidence discovered
in their *Four Plays or Moral Representations in One*
gives further proof of the importance of *Hamlet* merely
as a model for a revenge-tragedy; therefore, before dis-
cussing the two major works, let us consider this collection of four *Triumphs* consisting of a comedy, a tragi-
comedy, a tragedy, and a masque.

No resemblance to *Hamlet* appears until the note of
tragedy is heard, that is, in *The Triumph of Death*. Besides the usual verbal echoes that invariably accompany
the imitation of plot and character, we discover a second
Claudius in the villain Laval, to whom in the following
conversation between two courtiers all the vile traits of
the Danish usurper are attributed:

[1] See p. 5.

SECOND COURTIER.   For if Fame lye not
   He is *untemperate*.
FIRST COURTIER.   You express him poorly,
   Too gentle Sir: the most *deboist* and *barbarous*;
   Believe it, the most void of all humanity,
   Howe 'r *his cunning*, cloak it to his Uncle,
   And those his pride depends upon.
SECOND COURTIER.   I have heard too,
   Given excessively to drink.
FIRST COURTIER.   Most certain.
   And in that drink most dangerous . . .
                        Uncertain as the Sea, Sir,
   Proud and deceitful as his sins Great Master;
   His appetite to Women (for there he carries
   His main sail spread) *so boundles, and abominably*,
   That but to have her name by that tongue spoken,
   Poisons the virtue of the purest Virgin.[1]

                               (X, pp. 337-8)

Evidently Laval's chief vice is incontinence, for no sooner has he secretly married Gabriella than he casts her off in order to pursue Helena. A courtier invited to Helena's wedding questions the bridegroom's recent interest in the now forlorn Gabriella:

                      She is gone then,
   Or any else, that *promises, or power*,
   Gifts, or his *guilful vows* can work upon.[2]

                                (X, p. 338)

[1] Cf. J. Q. Adams, *Hamlet*, pp. 182-3.
[2] Cf. GHOST.   That incestuous, that adulterate beast,
     With witchcraft of his wit, with traitorous gifts—
     O wicked wit and gifts, that have the power
     So to seduce!—won to his shameful lust
     The will of my most seeming-virtuous queen.
                               (I. v. 42-6)

The libertine's methods thus approximate those of the villain who with "wicked wit and gifts" seduced the Queen of Denmark. Then Gabriella herself, cursing her successor in his affections, adds the final touch to the portrait, and we at once recognize Laval's resemblance to Claudius:

> Adders be your embraces.
> The poison of a rotten heart, oh Hellen!
> Blast thee as I have been; *just such a flattery,*
> *With that same cunning face, that smile upon 't,*
> Oh mark it Marie, mark it seriously,
> *That Master smile caught me.*[1]
>
> (X, pp. 338-9)

When Gabriella eventually decides to wipe out her disgrace by killing her faithless husband, her former lover Perolot, whom Laval falsely reported dead, appears on the scene and offers his aid. Her plan—

> To make his death more horrid (for he shall dye) . . .
> We'll watch him till he wakes,
> Then bind him, and then torture him—

he scornfully rejects:

>   'Tis nothing.
> No, *take him dead drunk now without repentance,*
> *His leachery inseam'd upon him.*[2]
>
> (X, p. 351)

[1] Cf. HAMLET. O villain! villain! *smiling,* damned villain!
      My tables. Meet it is I set it down,
      That one may *smile, and smile,* and be a villain.
                       (I. v. 106-8)

[2] Cf. HAMLET. Up, sword; and know thou a more horrid hent!
      When he is drunk asleep, or in his rage,
      Or in the incestuous pleasure of his bed . . .
      Then trip him, that his heels may kick at heaven,

Shortly before Laval dies, when his Evil Spirit enters to warn him of his approaching end, the doomed man, recalling all his past sins, tries in vain to pray. In his agony of remorse, like Claudius, he thinks the mere attitude of prayer may "serve his turn":

> Oh! my afflicted soul: *I cannot pray;*
> And the least child that has but goodness in him
> May strike my head off; so stupid are my powers:
> *I'll lift mine eyes up though.*[1]

(X, p. 353)

The *Triumph of Death* then ends true to form with the piling up of the murdered bodies of most of the main characters.

Yet the influence of *Hamlet* upon Beaumont and Fletcher was by no means restricted to this miniature revenge-play. Two of the main characters in *Philaster*, the hero and the despotic King, and to some degree a third, the heroine Arethusa, find counterparts respectively in Hamlet, Claudius, and Ophelia. Philaster, heir to the throne of Sicily, is the virtuous son of a dead king

---

> And that his soul may be as damn'd and black
> As hell, whereto it goes!

(III. iii. 88 ff.)

> Nay, but to live
> In the rank sweat of an *enseamed* bed!

(III. iv. 91-2)

[1] Cf. KING.   *Pray can I not:*
> Though inclination be as sharp as will,
> My stronger guilt defeats my strong intent;
> And, like a man to double business bound,
> I stand in pause where I shall first begin,
> And both neglect . . .
>   Then, *I'll look up;*
> My fault is past.

(*Hamlet*, III. iii. 38 ff.)

whose throne has been usurped by the King of Calabria.
The courtiers all recognize Philaster's claim to the crown
and his qualifications in general. Dion, the most important in the Court refers to him as—

> the right Heir . . . living so vertuously . . . the peo-
> ple admiring the bravery of his mind, and lamenting
> his injuries . . . whose Father we all know, was by
> our late King of Calabria, unrighteously deposed from
> his fruitful Cicilie.

> (I, p. 76)

Unfortunately the young Prince does nothing but talk
about his wrongs; indeed, so boldly and bitterly does he
speak that his enemies, believing him mad, scarcely know
whether or not to fear him. For example, to his rival
Pharamond he says:

> This earth you tread upon
> (A dowry as you hope with this fair Princess,
> Whose memory I bow to) was not left
> By my dead Father (Oh, I had a Father)
> To your inheritance, and I up and living,
> *Having my self about me and my sword,*
> *The souls of all my name, and memories,*
> *These arms and some few friends,* besides the gods,
> To part so calmly with it, and sit still,
> And say I might have been! I tell thee Pharamond,
> When thou art King, look I be dead and rotten,
> And my name ashes.[1]

> (I, p. 80)

---

[1] Cf. HAMLET   I do not know
> Why yet I live to say "This thing's to do,"
> Sith I have *cause*, and *will*, and *strength*, and *means*,
> To do 't.

> (III. viii. 43-6)

Pharamond in amazement exclaims:

> He's mad beyond cure, mad!

Philaster, however, after he has thus lashed himself with idle words into a fury, is ashamed of his futility:

> No Sir, I am too tame,
> Too much a Turtle, a thing born without passion,
> A faint shadow, that every drunken cloud sails over,
> And makes nothing.
> (I, pp. 80-1; cf. *Hamlet*, II. ii. 581-6)

The King then reprimands him, and reminds him that he is under constant surveillance:

> Go to:
> Be more your self, as you respect our favour:
> You 'l stir us else: Sir, I must have you know
> That y' are and shall be at our pleasure, what fashion we
> Will put upon you: smooth your brow, or by the gods—

The young man interrupts:

> I am dead Sir, y' are my fate: it was not I
> Said I was not wrong'd.

At this change of attitude the King wonderingly comments:

> Sure he 's possest.

Then with ambiguity much like that of Hamlet Philaster excuses his emotional display in a way that can serve only to increase the King's suspicions:

> Yes, with *my Fathers spirit*: It 's here O King!
> *A dangerous spirit;* now he tells me King,

> I was a Kings heir, bids me be a King,
> And whispers to me, these be all my Subjects.
> 'Tis strange, he will not let me sleep, but dives
> Into my fancy, and there gives me shapes
> That kneel, and do me service, cry me King:
> But *I 'le suppress him, he 's a factious spirit,*
> *And will undo me*: noble Sir, [your] hand, I am your
>   servant.[1]

 (I, p. 82; cf. *Hamlet*, II. ii. 615-20, also III. ii. 94-6)

But as Claudius is restrained from punishing Hamlet by—

> The great love the general gender bear him;
> Who, dipping all his faults in their affection,
> Would, like the spring that turneth wood to stone,
> Convert his gyves to graces—

          (IV. iii. 18-21)

so the King has to resign himself to the presence of Philaster, who also is beloved by the people. In reply to Cleremont's query—

> Sir, my ignorance in State-policy, will not let me know why Philaster being Heir to one of these King-doms, the King should suffer him to walk abroad with such free liberty—

Dion explains:

> The King (of late) made a hazard of both the King-doms, of Cicilie and his own, with offering but to im-prison Philaster. At which the City was in arms, not

---

[1] Cf. HAMLET.   *The spirit that I have seen*
> *May be the devil:* and the devil hath power
> To assume a pleasing shape; yea, and perhaps
> Out of my weakness, and my melancholy . . .
> *Abuses me to damn me.*

         (II. ii. 615 ff.)

to be charm'd down by any State-order or Proclamation, till they saw Philaster ride through the streets pleas'd and without a guard; at which they threw their Hats, and their arms from them; some to make bonefires, some to drink, all for his deliverance.

(I, p. 76)

His popularity with the common people is again evident in Cleon's criticism of his inaction:

> Philaster is too backward in 't himself;
> The Gentry do await it, and the people
> Against their nature are all bent for him,
> And like a field of standing Corn, that 's mov'd
> With a stiff gale, their heads bow all one way.

(I, p. 104)

But Cleon's comment also reveals that Philaster has the advantage of Hamlet in that the "gentry" are on his side. Even the Princess Arethusa is aware of the sentiment of the Court:

> You are all of his Faction; the whole Court
> Is bold in praise of him.

(I, p. 85)

And Dion and Cleremont, two courtiers whose high rank enables them to speak with authority, disclose their views directly to Philaster. Meeting him they inquire:

> How do you worthy Sir?

He replies:

> Well, very well;
> And so well, that if the King please, I find
> I may live many years.

At once Dion assures him:

> The King must please,
> Whilst *we* know what you are, and who you are,
> Your wrongs and your [injuries].
>
> (I, p. 83)

Later Dion goes so far as to inform Philaster that public sentiment has turned against the King:

> My good Lord,
> We come to urge that vertue which we know
> Lives in your breast, forth, rise, and make a head,
> The Nobles, and the people are all dull'd
> With this usurping King: and not a man
> That ever heard the word, or knew such a thing
> As vertue, but will second your attempts.

Philaster, however, postpones action:

> My designs
> Are not yet ripe, suffice it, that ere long
> I shall imploy your loves: but yet the time is short
> of what I would.

Though confident of the justice of his cause, through thinking too precisely on the event he does nothing. Like Hamlet, he pretends to doubt the authenticity of his father's "factious spirit." In order to inform the audience that the young man's delay is not only unnecessary but even dangerous, Dion warns him:

> The time is fuller Sir, than you expect;
> That which hereafter will not perhaps be reach'd
> By violence, may now be caught.
>
> (I, pp. 104-5)

Another Prince with a "motive and a cue for passion" thus lets go by the performance of his father's dread command.

Philaster's problems are further complicated by the foul slander cast upon his beloved Arethusa. His denunciation of the innocent girl resembles Hamlet's farewell to Ophelia, also falsely suspected of unchastity, in that Philaster, like Hamlet, first berates the individual woman and then proceeds to rail against women in general:

> Do I
> Bear all this bravely, and must sink at length
> Under a womans falshood? . . .
>   Some far place
> Where never womankind durst set her foot,
> For bursting with her poisons, must I seek,
> And live to curse you;
> There dig a Cave, and preach to birds and beasts,
> What woman is, and help to save them from you.
> How heaven is in your eyes, but in your hearts,
> More hell than hell has; how your tongues like Scorpions,
> Both heal and poyson . . .
> So farewel all my wo, all my delight.
>   (I, pp. 114-5; cf. *Hamlet*, III. i. 136 ff.)

When the King learns of the gross immorality of his prospective son-in-law, Prince Pharamond, and feels the need of divine assistance, he finds himself confronted by the same problem that troubled Claudius:

> You gods I see, that who unrighteously
> Holds wealth or state from others, shall be curst,
> In that, which meaner men are blest withall . . .

> Yet, if it be your wills, forgive the sin
> I have committed, let it not fall
> Upon this understanding child of mine,
> She has not broke your Laws; *but how can I,*
> *Look to be heard of gods, that must be just,*
> *Praying upon the ground I hold by wrong?*[1]

(I, p. 99)

Sustaining the resemblance, at the loss of the Princess the King displays an ignorance of divine law as profound as that of Claudius, who considers a bent knee sufficient for repentance. As Dion puts it, he "articles with the gods":

> I have sin'd 'tis true, and here stand to be punish'd;
> Yet would not thus be punish'd; *let me chuse*
> *My way, and lay it on.*

(I, p. 122; cf. *Hamlet*, III. iii. 70-2)

Amintor, the hero of *The Maids Tragedy*, also finds his prototype in the Dane. He typifies, something like Hamlet, the Elizabethan concept of the complete gentleman. His wife refers to his "fair soul" and his "noble youth,"[2] and even his arch-enemy, the King, compliments him:

> Is not his spirit,
> Though he be temperate, of a valiant strain,
> As this our age hath known?

(I, p. 32)

---

[1] Cf. KING.
> But, O! *what form of prayer*
> *Can serve my turn?* "Forgive me my foul murder"?
> *That cannot be, since I am still possess'd*
> *Of those effects* for which I did the murder,
> My crown, mine own ambition, and my queen.
> (*Hamlet*, III. iii. 51-5)

[2] I, pp. 50-1; cf. *Hamlet*, I. v. 38.

Brave soldier though he is, his horror at his wife's adulterous relationship with the King is so intense that all his
courage is sicklied o'er with the pale cast of thought.
His bosom friend Melantius tactfully tries to discover the
cause of his grief:

> I have observ'd, *your words fall from your tongue*
> *Wildly;* and all your carriage,
> Like one that strove to shew his merry mood,
> When he were ill dispos'd . . .
> 'Tis not your nature
> To be thus idle; I have seen you stand
> As you were blasted; midst of all your mirth,
> Call thrice aloud, and then start, feigning joy
> So coldly![1]

(I, pp. 36-7)

At first his inaction seems to belie the King's description
of him and impresses us as cowardice, but before long
it becomes clear that his will is so paralyzed with ab-
horrence at his wife's sin that he cannot act. He is able
only to work his brain into a fever over the problem
confronting him in the conflict between his duty to the
King and his right as a husband. As a result of his
melancholia, he contemplates suicide, and Melantius expresses the fear that his friend may "do violence upon
himself."[2]

Although Melantius, thus loyal to Amintor and eager
to aid him in obtaining revenge, resembles Horatio, he

[1] Cf. Horatio to Hamlet:
These are but *wild* and *whirling words*, my lord.
(I. v. 133)
[2] I, p. 42. See J. Q. Adams, *Hamlet*, p. 196, for his discussion of
Hamlet in a similar situation.

also calls to mind Laertes. Just as Laertes and Hamlet find themselves in similar situations, their fathers supposedly murdered by the same man, so Melantius and Amintor face a common enemy in the King, who has seduced Evadne, the sister of one and the wife of the other. Again, although Hamlet hesitates, Laertes, husbanding his scant means, pushes on to his revenge; similarly, while Amintor, who has suffered the greater wrong, merely bemoans his fate, Melantius no sooner hears of Evadne's sin than he cries:

> From his Iron Den I 'le waken death,
> And hurle him on this King; my honesty
> Shall steel my sword, and on its horrid point
> I 'le wear my cause, that shall amaze the eyes
> Of this proud man.
>
> (I, p. 40; cf. Hamlet, IV. i. 130-5)

And he promptly sets about his task.

Polonius finds a close counterpart in Calianax, an old Lord and friend to the King. The talkative old man's description of himself might have come from the lips of the Danish Counsellor:

> To say the truth,
> However I may set a face, and talk,
> I am not valiant: when I was a youth,
> I kept my credit with a testie trick I had
> Amongst cowards, but durst never fight.
>
> (I, p. 35)

He spends most of his time meddling in the affairs of others, especially those of his daughter. His relationship to Polonius is also brought out by means of verbal echoes,

particularly in the scene where he tries in vain to betray
Melantius to the King, who answers only:

> Well, *I will try him*, and if this be true,
> I 'le pawn my life, I 'le find it; if 't be false,
> And that you clothe your hate in such a lie,
> You shall hereafter *doat in your own house*, not in the
> Court.

Highly insulted, Calianax cries:

> Why if it be a lie,
> Mine ears are false; for I 'le be sworn I heard it:
> Old men are good for nothing; you were best
> *Put me to death for hearing*, and free him
> For meaning of it; *you would ha' trusted me
> Once*, but the time is altered.[1]

> (I, p. 52)

The resemblance between the two dotards is increased
by the fact that Calianax has a daughter, Aspatia, who
suffers disappointment in love. Until Amintor deserts
her, she believes herself loved by him:

[1] POLONIUS. Hath there been such a time—I'd fain know that—
That I have positively said, "'Tis so,"
When it prov'd otherwise?
KING.   Not that I know.
POLONIUS. *Take this from this, if this be otherwise.*
If circumstances lead me, I will find
Where truth is hid, though it were hid indeed
Within the centre!
KING.   How may we *try* it further? . . .
We will try it.

> (II. ii. 153 ff.)

HAMLET. [*of* Polonius] Let the doors be shut upon him, *that he
may play the fool no where but in 's own house.*

> (III. i. 133-4)

> Perhaps he found me worthless,
> But till he did so, in these ears of mine,
> (These credulous ears) he pour'd the sweetest words
> That Art or Love could frame.
>
> (I, p. 15; cf. *Hamlet*, I. iii. 110 ff.)

Afterward she becomes dejected and seeks the "unfrequented woods" where she has her maids gather wild flowers and "strow her over like a corse" while she sings "the mournful'st things that ever ear hath heard."[1] Her conversation with the guilty Evadne recalls Ophelia's ambiguous replies to the Queen. As the forlorn maid attends her successful rival for Amintor's love, she interrupts the merry conversation of the other ladies-in-waiting:

> Lay a Garland on my Hearse of the dismal Yew.

Evadne tries to soothe her:

> That's one of your sad songs Madam.

The other replies:

> Believe me, 'tis a very pretty one.

Desiring to humor her, Evadne asks:

> How is it Madam?

Then Aspatia sings:

> Lay a Garland on my Hearse of the dismal yew;
> Maidens, Willow branches bear; say I died true:
> My Love was false, but I was firm from my hour of birth;
> Upon my buried body lay lightly gentle earth.
>
> (I, p. 16; cf. *Hamlet*, IV. i. 21 ff.)

[1] I, p. 4; cf. *Hamlet*, IV. iii. 165-82.

Evadne's resemblance to Gertrude is more clearly brought out in the Fourth Act in her conversation with her brother Melantius, which closely parallels the closet scene. Both women are guilty of adultery with a villainous King. Although Melantius is seeking the name of his sister's seducer, whereas Hamlet has already ascertained his mother's companion in sin, both are equally direct in their accusations. When at first put off by a pretense of injured virtue on the part of the adulteress, neither is deceived. Each at once proceeds to shower threats and insults upon the head of the accused and ends by persuading the sinner to repentance.

Melantius, entering his sister's chamber, greets her, and scarcely noticing her reply plunges immediately into his business:

In my blunt eye methinks you look Evadne—

As he pauses, she prompts him:

Come, you would make me blush.

He answers:

I would Evadne, I shall displease my ends else.

Then locking the door he continues:

They that commit thy faults, fly the remembrance.

But, like Gertrude, she refuses to understand him:

My faults, Sir! I would have you know I care not
If they were written here, here in my forehead.

Nothing daunted, he speaks more clearly:

Thy body is too little for the story,
The lusts of which would fill another woman,
Though she had Twins within her.

She moves to dismiss him:

> This is saucy;
> Look you intrude no more, there lies your way.

Shocked by her brazen impudence, he goes straight to the point. Grasping her arm he cries:

> I come to know that desperate Fool that drew thee
> From thy fair life; be wise, and lay him open.

Struggling in his grasp, but still stubborn, she exclaims:

> Unhand me, and learn manners, such another
> Forgetfulness forfeits your life.

At this remark he bursts forth into brutal denunciation:

> Quench me this mighty humour, and then tell me
> Whose Whore you are, for you are one, I know it . . .
> The burnt air, when the Dog raigns, is not fouler
> Than thy contagious name, till thy repentance
> (If the Gods grant thee any) purge thy sickness.

Still she believes that she can force him to drop the issue:

> Be gone, you are my Brother, that's your safety.

He disclaims the bond:

> I 'le be a Wolf first; 'tis to be thy Brother
> An infamy below the sin of a Coward:
> *I am as far from being part of thee,*
> *As thou art from thy vertue.*[1]

As she remains obdurate, he rushes on:

> I would speak loud; here's one should *thunder* to
> 'em . . .
> Thou hast death about thee: h'as undone thine honour,

[1] Cf. *Hamlet*, III. iv. 14-7.

poyson'd thy vertue, and *of a lovely rose, left thee a
canker* . . .

Speak you whore, speak truth,
Or by the dear soul of thy sleeping Father,
This sword shall be thy lover: tell, or I 'le kill thee:
And when thou hast told all, thou wilt deserve it.[1]

Terror-stricken Evadne cries:

You will not murder me! . . . Help![2]

Finally, when she breaks down and admits her guilt, he
asks with some gentleness:

How long have you liv'd thus Evadne?

In remorse she answers:

Too long.

Seeing her thus repentant he continues:

Too late you find it: can you be sorry?

She replies:

Would I were half as blameless.

Then he warns her:

Evadne, thou wilt to thy trade again.

[1] Cf. HAMLET. Such an act
That blurs the grace and blush of modesty!
*Calls virtue hypocrite! takes off the rose
From the fair forehead of an innocent love
And sets a blister there!* . . .
QUEEN. Ay me, what act,
That roars so loud and *thunders* in the index.
(III. iv. 40 ff.)

[2] Cf. QUEEN. What wilt thou do? *Thou wilt not murder me?
Help, help, ho!*
(III. iv. 21-2)

But she assures him:

> First to my grave.

Both Philaster and Amintor, then, are placed in situations similar to those in which Hamlet finds himself, and they react much as he did. Philaster has been deprived of his lawful inheritance, yet with plenty of opportunity he postpones action. Amintor's attitude toward his wife's relationship with the King duplicates Hamlet's horror at his mother's infidelity, and neither youth is able to summon energy enough to punish the offenders. In addition, each hero in Beaumont and Fletcher is surrounded by persons who have their counterparts in the Shakespearean play: in *Philaster*, the King for Claudius, Arethusa for Ophelia; and in *The Maids Tragedy*, Melantius for Horatio, Calianax for Polonius, Aspatia for Ophelia, and Evadne for Gertrude.

Thus do Beaumont and Fletcher, like the other dramatists, turn directly to Shakespeare for inspiration; and further evidence of their imitation of *Hamlet* appears in later chapters.

V

IMITATIONS OF CHARACTERS FROM
HAMLET

I N CERTAIN plays the imitation is restricted to some
outstanding quality, either inherent or accidental, of
a particular character in *Hamlet*, and hence only to those
scenes in which that quality reveals itself. A playwright
wishing to depict disillusionment frequently takes as a
model the Prince himself. Again, in portraying the incon-
stant wife he thinks of Gertrude, and often imitates those
scenes in which her infidelity is most apparent, as the
Mouse-Trap scene where her fickleness is satirized, or
the closet scene where she is accused of her sin. And
we may often detect reminiscences of Ophelia in some
forsaken maid driven insane as a result of a lover's
cruelty.

Like Hamlet, Captain Ager, in *A Fair Quarrel*
(Thomas Middleton, 1617), "thinks too precisely on the
event." When the lying Colonel slanders Ager's mother,
the Captain at once challenges him to a duel. They are
unable to fight, however, because their swords have
been removed by Ager's uncle, who has foreseen the
possibility of such a quarrel. When Ager next appears,
his normal healthy energy has dissipated itself in doubt,
and he gives vent to his thoughts in a long soliloquy.
At the beginning of his meditation he seems fully aware
of the justice of his cause:

> If it were possible
> That souls could fight after the bodies fell,
> This was a quarrel for 'em.

But his next words indicate that—if we may borrow
from Hamlet's description of himself in a similar state
of mind—his native hue of resolution is becoming sicklied
o'er with the pale cast of thought:

> He should be one, indeed,
> That never heard of heaven's joys or hell's torments
> To fight this out: *I am too full of conscience,*
> Knowledge, and patience, to give justice to 't;
> *So careful of my eternity,* which consists
> Of upright actions, that *unless I knew*
> *It were a truth I stood for, any coward*
> *Might make my breast his foot-pace:* and who lives
> That can assure the truth of his conception
> More than a mother's carriage makes it hopeful?[1]

His mind, dwelling on his problem in this way, gives
him an excuse for delay. Notwithstanding his initial conviction of his mother's innocence, he now tells himself
in language bordering upon rant that he needs further
proof:

> And is 't not miserable valour then
> That man should hazard all upon things doubtful?
> O, there 's the cruelty of my foe 's advantage!
> Could but my soul *resolve my cause were just,*

[1] Cf. HAMLET. But that the dread of *something after death,*
> The undiscover'd country, from whose bourn
> No traveller returns, *puzzles the will,*
> And makes us rather bear those ills we have
> Than fly to others that we know not of?
> *Thus conscience does make cowards of us all.*
> (III. i. 78-83)

> Earth's mountain nor sea's surge should hide him from
>   me!
> E'en *to hell's threshold would I follow him,*
> *And see the slanderer in before I left him!*[1]

Then he suddenly remembers that never before has he
been so particular about facts. In the past, indeed, where
"honor was at the stake"—again to borrow from *Hamlet*—he has always "found quarrel in a straw":

> But as it is, it fears me; and I never
> Appear'd too conscionably just till now.

And, like Hamlet, he reiterates his expression of confidence in his mother's honor:

> My good opinion of her life and virtues
> Bids me go on, and fain would I be rul'd by 't.[2]

He excuses himself, however, by saying that like all
women his mother is frail:

> But when my judgment tells me she's *but woman;*
> Whose *frailty* let in death to all mankind,
> My valour shrinks at that.[3]

Nevertheless he has the grace summarily to dismiss this
fear as groundless—

> Certain, she's good—

>   (II. i. 5-30)

and he finally decides to go directly to his mother.

At that point she enters. At first she angrily denounces

---

[1] Cf. *Hamlet,* III. iii. 73 ff.
[2] Cf. *Hamlet,* III. viii. 43-6.
[3] Cf. HAMLET. *Frailty,* thy name is "*woman.*"

                                         (I. ii. 146)

him for failing to leap to the defense of her reputation; but when she realizes that he may be killed, in order to shield him she tells him that she was by a kinswoman "betray'd to a most sinful hour." Horrified at the thought, he exclaims:

> False! do not say 't, for honour's goodness, do not!
> You never could be so. He I call'd father
> Deserv'd you at your best, when youth and merit
> Could boast at highest in you; y' had no grace
> Or virtue that he match'd not, no delight
> That you invented but he sent it crown'd
> To your full-wishing soul.
>   (II. i. 189-95; cf. *Hamlet*, I. v. 47-50)

Then, just as Hamlet becomes melancholy at the knowledge of his mother's infidelity, Ager loses all interest in life:

> I should be dead, for all my life's work 's ended.
>   (II. i. 211)

He ignores the appeals of his friends and submits to the indignities heaped upon him by the Colonel and his companions. Then the Colonel makes the mistake of calling Ager a "base submissive coward," whereupon Ager fights the duel. When he returns home victorious, his mother reassures him of her virtue.

Also resembling Shakespeare's young Prince is Charalois, the sensitive, courteous hero of *The Fatal Dowry* (Philip Massinger, 1619) who delays in securing "the decent rites of burial" for his dead father. Massinger's hero himself discloses that, like Hamlet, he is both scholar and soldier:

Declare this foe of mine, and life's, that like
A man I may encounter and subdue it.
It shall not have one such effect in me,
As thou denouncest: with a *soldier's* arm,
If it be strength, I'll meet it; if a fault
Belonging to my mind, I'll cut it off
With mine own reason, as a *scholar* should.

(I, p. 417; cf. *Hamlet*, III. i. 155-6)

The resemblance is more evident in the scene in which Charalois, dressed in garments of deep mourning, stands patiently listening to his friends who urge him to cast aside his "sable habit." Since his father's creditors intend to retain the corpse of the dead man, immediate action is necessary. Romont is the first to try to arouse Charalois from his lethargy:

Heaven! you weep:
And I could do so too, but that I know
There's more expected from the son and friend
Of him whose fatal loss now shakes our natures,
Than sighs or tears.[1]

(III, p. 365)

Later another friend Rochfort gives similar advice:

Fie, no more of this!
You have outwept a woman, noble Charalois.
No man but has or must bury a father.

(III, p. 395; cf. *Hamlet*, I. ii. 89-94)

[1] Cf. HAMLET. What may this mean,
That thou, dead corse, again in complete steel
Revisit'st thus the glimpses of the moon,
Making night hideous, and we fools of nature
So horridly to shake our disposition
With thoughts beyond the reaches of our souls?

(I. iv. 51-6)

Further like Hamlet, Charalois suffers disillusionment in a woman dear to him. His exclamation upon discovering his wife's infidelity echoes Hamlet's dazed words after the Ghost has disclosed Gertrude's secret shame:

> Oh *my heart!*
> *Hold* yet a little.[1]

(III, p. 435)

An even more obvious imitation of young Hamlet appears in *The Lover's Melancholy* (John Ford, 1628), in which Palador's melancholia baffles the Court of Cyprus during the greater part of the play. Ford's hero also is the expectancy and rose of the fair state. His idealistic nature reveals itself in his expression of admiration for—

> *man*, the abstract
> Of all perfection, *which the workmanship*
> *Of heaven hath modell'd.*[2]

(I, p. 83)

At the beginning of the play, however, he is not himself. His cousin Amethus informs us that—

> He's the same melancholy man
> He was at's father's death; sometimes speaks sense
> But seldom mirth; will smile, but seldom laugh;
> Will lend an ear to business, deal in none.

(I, p. 12)

---

[1] Cf. HAMLET.   *Hold, hold, my heart!*

(I. v. 93)

[2] Cf. HAMLET. What a *piece of work is a man*! How noble in reason! how infinite in faculty! in form, in moving, how express and admirable! in action how like an angel! in apprehension how like a god! the beauty of the world!

(II. ii. 310-14)

His mental depression results chiefly from the disappearance of his betrothed Eroclea, the daughter of the Chief Counsellor of the kingdom. As the action progresses, he learns much to his sorrow that his own father had attempted to seduce her, whereupon she had fled from the Court, no one knows whither. Consequently Palador, like Hamlet, suffers not only the loss of a loved one but also disillusionment in a parent; and in both men the ensuing grief induces melancholia.

The courtiers all wonder at Palador's dejection, and Corax, his chief physician, takes it upon himself to ascertain the cause thereof. Like Polonius, he boasts that—

> I will discover whence his sadness is,
> Or undergo the censure of my ignorance.
> <div align="right">(I, p. 53; cf. <i>Hamlet</i>, II. ii. 46-9)</div>

The royal tutor Aretus also expresses his determination to analyze the Prince's abnormal behavior:

> Passions of violent nature, by degrees
> Are easiliest reclaim'd. *There's something hid
> Of his distemper*, which we'll now find out.

A few moments after Aretus speaks, Palador enters "with a book."[1] As soon as the Prince perceives that every-

---

[1] I, pp. 29-30; cf.—

> KING. He tells me, my sweet queen, that he hath found
> The head and source of all your son's *distemper* . . .
> (II. ii. 54 ff.)

A little further on appears the stage direction—
> *Enter* Hamlet, *reading on a book.*

Cf. also—KING.   *There's something in his soul*
> O'er which his melancholy sits on brood.
> (III. i. 169-70)

one is trying to pluck out the heart of his mystery, he
takes his friend Rhetias to one side and begs:

> O, be faithful,
> And let no *politick lord* work from thy bosom
> My griefs: I know thou wert put on to *sift* me;
> But be not too secure . . .
> Continue still thy discontented fashion;
> Humour the lords, as they would humour me;
> I 'll not live in thy debt.[1]

(I, p. 37)

Finally he turns on his inquisitors:

> Ye have consented all to work upon
> The softness of my nature; but take heed:
> Though I can sleep in silence, and look on
> The mockery ye make of my dull patience,
> Yet ye shall know, the best of ye, that in me
> There is a masculine, a stirring spirit,
> Which, [once] provok'd, shall, like a bearded comet,
> Set ye at gaze, and threaten horror.[2]

(I, p. 82)

Before the end of the play, however, Eroclea is restored
to him, and his melancholia vanishes.

The character of the faithless Gertrude must have
fascinated John Marston, for both Celia (*What You
Will*, 1601) and Isabella (*The Insatiate Countess*, 1610),
in addition to Maria whom we have already discussed,[3]

---

[1] Cf. Hamlet's adjuration to Horatio and Marcellus (I. v. 169 ff.);
also II. ii. 47 and

KING. Well, we shall *sift* him.

(II. ii. 58)

[2] Cf. Hamlet to Rosencrantz and Guildenstern (III. ii. 373 ff.);
also III. ii. 393.

[3] See pp. 20-2.

resemble the Danish Queen. Celia's sudden marriage "scarce three months"[1] after hearing of the drowning of her husband Albano, provokes much adverse criticism. Informed of her faithlessness, Albano sadly asks his servant:

> Is 't possible I should be dead so soon
> In her affects? How long is 't since our shipwrack?
>
> (III. ii. 6-7)

Slip replies:

> 'Tis just three months.
> Shall I speak like a poet?—*thrice hath the horned moon*—[2]

But Albano interrupts him:

> Talk not of horns.

Then he describes his wife's innumerable protestations of fidelity:

> O Celia! How oft,
> When thou hast laid thy cheek upon my breast,
> And with lascivious petulancy sued
> For hymeneal dalliance, marriage-rites;—
> O then, how oft, with passionate protests
> And zealous vows, hast thou obliged thy love,
> In *dateless bands*, unto Albano's breast!
> Then, *did I but mention second marriage,*
> *With what a bitter hate would she inveigh*

---

[1] I. i. 205; cf. *Hamlet*, I. ii. 138:
    But *two months dead!* nay, not so much, not two!
[2] Cf. PLAYER KING. And *thirty dozen moons* with borrow'd sheen
    About the world have times twelve thirties been.
                                            (III. ii. 161-2)

'Gainst retail'd wedlocks! "O!" would she lisp,
"*If you should die*,"—then would she slide a tear,
And with a wanton languishment intwist
Her hands,—"*O God, and you should die! Marry?*
Could I love life, my dear Albano dead?
Should any prince possess his widow's bed?"
And now, see, see, I am but rumour'd drown'd?[1]

(III. ii. 17-34)

A more impressive imitation of Gertrude, however, we find in the Insatiate Countess, who at the opening of the play is mourning the recent death of her husband. For Count Roberto, who comes to console her, she at first has only a rebuke:

My lord of Cyprus, *do not mock my grief.*
Tears are as due a tribute to the dead,
As fear to God, and duty unto kings,
Love to the just, or hate unto the wicked.[2]

(I. i. 34-7)

---

[1] Cf. *Hamlet*, I. ii. 143-5; also—

PLAYER KING. Since love our hearts and Hymen did our hands
Unite commutual in most *sacred bands* . . .
And thou shalt live in this fair world behind,
Honour'd, belov'd; and haply, one as kind
For husband shalt thou—
PLAYER QUEEN. *O, confound the rest!*
Such love must needs be treason in my breast.
In second husband let me be accurst!
None wed the second but who kill'd the first . . .
A second time I kill my husband dead
When second husband kisses me in bed!

(III. ii. 163 ff.)

[2] HORATIO. My lord, I came to see your father's funeral.
HAMLET. I pray thee, *do not mock me*, fellow-student.

(I. ii. 176-7)

Nevertheless he continues:

> Surcease;
> *Believe it is a wrong unto the gods.*
> *They sail against the wind that wail the dead:*
> And since his heart hath wrestled with death's pangs,
> *From whose stern cave none tracts a backward path,*
> Leave to lament this necessary change,
> And thank the gods, for they can do us good.[1]
>
> (I. i. 38-44)

But Isabella's grief is mere show, for even before the Count leaves her, she consents to marry him. Then, as in *Hamlet*, because of a woman's inconstancy marriage festivities immediately follow funeral rites.

The Countess' unseemly haste provokes one of the courtiers to comment:

> A *player's passion* I'll believe hereafter,
> And in a tragic scene weep for *old Priam*,
> When *fell-revenging Pyrrhus* with supposed
> And artificial wounds mangles his breast,
> And think it a more worthy act to me,
> Than trust a female mourning o'er her love.[2]
>
> (I. i. 121-6)

---

[1] Cf. KING.   *'Tis a fault to heaven,*
> A fault against the dead, a fault to nature,
> To reason most absurd.
>
> (I. ii. 101-3)

> HAMLET. The undiscover'd country, *from whose bourn*
> *No traveller returns* . . .
>
> (III. i. 79-80)

[2] Cf. FIRST PLAYER.   Unequal match'd
> *Pyrrhus at Priam drives;* in rage strikes wide;
> But with the whiff and wind of his *fell* sword
> The unnerved father falls.
>
> (II. ii. 483-6)

Another bystander jeers:

> Learn of a well-composèd epigram
> A woman's love, and thus 'twas sung unto us;
>
>> The tapers that stood on her husband's hearse
>>   Isabel advances to a second bed:
>> Is it not wondrous strange for to rehearse
>>   She should so soon forget her husband, *dead*
>> *One hour? for if the husband's life once fade*
>> *Both love and husband in one grave are laid.*[1]
>>
>>   (I. i. 130-7)

Soon tiring of Roberto, she deserts him for a third. Completely disillusioned, he describes her fulsome display of affection in terms that recall Hamlet's first soliloquy:

> Who would have thought it? She that could no more
> Forsake my company than can the day
> Forsake the glorious presence of the sun!—
> When I was absent then *her gallèd eyes*
> Would have shed April showers, and outwept
> The clouds in that same o'er-passionate mood,

Cf. also the lines in Hamlet's second soliloquy referring to the First Player:

HAMLET. Is it not monstrous that this *player* here,
    But in a fiction, in a dream of *passion*,
    Could force his soul so to his own conceit,
    That from her working all his visage wann'd.
                          (II. ii. 565-8)

[1] Cf. *Hamlet*, I. ii. 180-1; also
    . . . for, look you how cheerfully my mother looks, and
    my father *died within's two hours!*
                          (III. ii. 128-30)
    So think thou wilt no second husband wed;
    But *die thy thoughts when thy first lord is dead.*
                          (III. ii. 218-9)

> When they drowned all the world, yet now forsakes
> me!
>
> (II. iv. 30-6)

> *She had a lord*
> *Jealous the air would ravish her chaste looks.*[1]
>
> (V. i. 169-70)

Eventually, however, she goes mad, and, as a final remi-
niscence of the earlier play entirely apart from the theme
of conjugal infidelity but quite as indicative of Shakespeare's hold upon contemporary writers, she comes
upon the stage like Ophelia, "her hair hanging down, a
chaplet of flowers on her head, and a nosegay in her
hand."

In *The Widow's Tears* (George Chapman, 1605), the
theme of which is the infidelity of wives, Chapman
seems to have in mind Gertrude, and hence the Player
Queen, in his portrayal of both the Widow Countess
and Cynthia. The Countess protests that she will never
remarry, but quickly forgets her vow. Her ostentatious
fidelity to her former husband is thus described by her
lady-in-waiting:

> I have been witness to so many of her fearful protesta-
> tions to our late lord against that course; to her infinite
> oaths imprinted on his lips, and sealed in his heart with
> such imprecations to her bed, if ever it should receive a
> second impression; to her open and often detestations of
> that incestuous life (as she termed it) of widows' mar-
> riages, as being but a kind of lawful adultery, like usury

[1] Cf. HAMLET.   So loving to my mother
>   *That he might not beteem the winds of heaven*
>   *Visit her face too roughly* . . .
>   Ere yet the salt of most unrighteous tears
>   Had left the flushing in *her galled eyes,*
>   She married.
>
> (I. ii. 140 ff.)

permitted by the law, not approv'd; that *to wed a second, was no better than to cuckold the first.*
(II. iv. 22-31; cf. *Hamlet*, I. ii. 143-6, also III. ii. 183-9)

When the cynical Tharsalio, doubting the sincerity of her protestations, expresses his determination to win her affections, his sister Cynthia reminds him:

But, brother, have I not heard you say your own ears have been witness to her vows, made solemnly to your late lord, in memory of him to preserve till death the unstained honour of a widow's bed? If nothing else, yet that might cool your confidence.

(I. i. 88-92)

He replies:

But pray, sister, tell me—you are a woman—do not you wives nod your heads and smile one upon another when ye meet abroad? . . . As who should say, "Are not we mad wenches, that can lead our blind husbands thus by the noses?" Do you not brag among your selves how grossly you abuse their honest credulities? . . . *How you vow widowhood in their lifetime* and they believe you, when *even in the sight of their breathless corse, ere they be fully cold, you join embraces with* his groom, or his physician, and *perhaps his poisoner; or at least, by the next moon* (if you can expect so long) solemnly plight new hymeneal bonds, with a wild, confident, untamed ruffian?[1]

(I. i. 101 ff.)

[1] Cf. PLAYER QUEEN. In second husband let me be accurst;
   None wed the second but who kill'd the first.

(III. ii. 183-4)

Yet both she and Gertrude "joined embraces" with their first husband's poisoner; Gertrude, indeed—

   within a month!
   Ere yet the salt of most unrighteous tears,
   Had left the flushing in her galled eyes.

(I. ii. 153-5)

But the boaster knows whereof he speaks. Upon learning of the Widow's capitulation, his brother-in-law Lysander exclaims:

> But let me wonder at this *frailty* yet;
> Would she in so short time wear out his memory,
> So soon wipe from her eyes, nay, from her heart,
> Whom I myself, and this whole isle besides,
> Still remember with grief, the impression of his loss
> Taking worthily such root in us;
> How think you, wife?[1]
>
> (III. i. 112-8)

Cynthia, who likewise protests too much, responds:

> I am asham'd on 't, and abhor to think
> So great and vow'd a pattern of our sex
> Should take into her thoughts, nay, to her bed,
> (O stain to womanhood!) a second love.

Her husband adds:

> In so short a time!

She declares:

> In any time!
>
> (III. i. 119-23)

For Cynthia, too, has vowed to marry only once:

> One temple seal'd our troth;
> One tomb, one hour shall end and shroud us both.
>
> (III. ii. 75-6)

In order to test her sincerity, Lysander, at Tharsalio's suggestion of course, has a false report of his death sent

---

[1] Cf. HAMLET. *Frailty*, thy name is "woman."

(I. ii. 146)

her. At first she makes a great show of grief and insists upon being buried alive with her husband. Tharsalio, however, is still skeptical:

> Her officious ostentation of sorrow condemns her sincerity. When did ever woman mourn so unmeasurably, but she did dissemble? . . . My sister may *turn Niobe* for love; but till Niobe be turned to a marble, I 'll not despair but she may prove *a woman.*[1]
>
> (IV. i. 110 ff.)

Then, as he anticipated, after only four days of mourning she gives herself to a common soldier, in reality her own husband in disguise. Poor Lysander consequently is utterly disillusioned. Concealing his identity, he assures his wife that she has indeed done all that was required of a mourning widow:

> Th'ast wept these four whole days.

Her maid corrects him:

> Nay, by 'r lady, almost five!

And Lysander comments:

> *Look you* there; near upon five whole days![2]
>
> (V. i. 110-2)

---

[1] Cf. HAMLET. A little month; or ere those shoes were old
      With which she follow'd my poor father's body,
      Like Niobe, all tears.

(I. ii. 147-9)

[2] Cf. HAMLET. What should a man do but be merry? for, *look you* how cheerfully my mother looks, and my father died *within's two hours*!

OPHELIA. *Nay, 'tis twice two months,* my lord.

HAMLET. *So long!*

(III. ii. 127-32)

Of the three most notable imitations of Ophelia—Lucibella in *Hoffman*,[1] Aspatia in *The Maids Tragedy*,[2] and Aphelia in *The Fatal Contract*[3]—only one, Lucibella, depends for at least part of her resemblance upon her insanity. Two other less detailed imitations, the Jailor's Daughter in *The Two Noble Kinsmen* (Beaumont and Fletcher, 1613) and Penthea in *The Broken Heart* (John Ford, 1629), have in common with the Shakespearean heroine little more than their madness caused by disappointed love.

The Jailor's Daughter out of love for Palamon frees him on condition that he will meet her in the woods and take her away with him. When he fails her, she loses her way and goes mad. In her frenzy her mind alternates between the danger in which her act has placed her father, the Jailor, and the loss of her lover. Her rejected suitor tells her father how she appeared when he found her:

> As I late was angling
> In the great Lake that lies behind the Palace,
> From the far shore, thick set with Reeds and Sedges,
> As patiently I was attending sport,
> I heard a voice, a shrill one, and attentive
> I gave my ear, when I might well perceive
> 'Twas one that sung, and by the smallness of it
> A Boy or Woman . . .
> I saw it was your Daughter . . .
> She sung much, but no sence; only I heard her
> Repeat this often. Palamon is gone,
> Is gone to th' wood to gather Mulberries,

[1] See pp. 25-7.
[2] See pp. 65-7.
[3] See pp. 45-7.

I 'll find him out to morrow . . .
                    Then she talk'd *of you, Sir;*
That you must lose your head to morrow morning
And she must gather Flowers to bury you,
And see the house made handsome, *then she sung*
Nothing but willow, willow, willow, and between
Ever was, *Palamon, fair Palamon,*
And Palamon, was a tall young man. The place
Was knee deep where she sate; her careless Tresses,
A wreath of Bull-rush rounded; about her stuck
Thousand fresh Water Flowers of several colours.
That methought she appear'd like the fair Nymph
That feeds the lake with waters, or as Iris
Newly dropt down from heaven; *Rings she made*
Of Rushes that grew by, and to 'em spoke
The prettiest posies: thus our true love's ty'd,
This you may loose, not me, and many a one:
And then she wept, *and sung again,* and sigh'd,
And with the same breath smil'd, and kist her hand.
(IX, pp. 348-9; cf. *Hamlet,* IV. iii. 165 ff., also IV. i.
23 ff.)

Here we have another Ophelia driven insane with
grief at her lover's unkindness. The Queen, relating the
circumstances of Ophelia's death, explains that the girl
in her effort to hang her "coronet weeds" on the pend-
ent boughs of a *willow* tree fell in the weeping brook
where—

                    Her clothes spread wide,
And, *mermaid-like,* awhile they bore her up;
Which time *she chanted snatches of old tunes,*
As one incapable of her own distress,
Or like a creature native and indu'd
Unto that element.

                            (IV. iii. 174-9)

Similarly, the suitor compares the Jailor's Daughter as she sits in the lake weaving garlands from rushes and singing "nothing but willow, willow, willow" to "the fair nymph that feeds the lake with waters." The forsaken maid in Beaumont and Fletcher, however, is rescued, and when she reappears, sustaining her resemblance to Ophelia in an earlier scene, she talks of her approaching marriage and sings snatches of songs:

> I have forgot it quite; the burden on 't was *Down A Down a.*[1]

> (IX, p. 356)

Penthea bears even a closer resemblance to the heroine of *Hamlet*. Because her ambitious brother has forced her to give up her true love Orgilus and marry the jealous Bassanes, she goes mad. In her distraction she dwells first on her father's death and then on her broken betrothal:

> You may live well, and die a good old man:
> By yea and nay, an oath not to be broken,
> *If you had join'd our hands once in the temple,—*
> *'Twas since my father died,* for had he liv'd
> He would have done 't.

> (I, p. 293; cf. *Hamlet*, IV. i. 182-5)

At the same time she indicates to her former suitor that her brother Ithocles is the cause of her seeming faithlessness:

[1] Cf. OPHELIA. You must sing, "*A-down a-down!*" and you, "*Call him a-down-a!*"

(IV. i. 169-70)

Also like Ophelia, the Jailor's Daughter occasionally intersperses obscenity among her songs.

I loved you once . . . [*To* Orgilus.
Goodness! we had been happy; too much happiness
Will make folk proud, they say—but that is he—
                         [*Pointing to* Ithocles.
And yet he paid for 't home; alas, his heart
Is crept into the cabinet of the princess;
We shall have points and bride-laces. Remember,
When we last gather'd roses in the garden,
I found my wits; but truly you lost yours.
That's he, and still 'tis he.
                     [*Again pointing to* Ithocles.

Although to Ithocles her words are meaningless—

                     Poor soul, how idly
Her fancies guide her tongue—

to Orgilus she presents a "document in madness":

                     She has tutor'd me;
Some powerful inspiration checks my laziness . . .
If this be madness, madness is an oracle.[1]
                         (I, pp. 291-2)

    Another imitation of the mad Ophelia not connected
with disappointed love occurs in *The White Devil*
(John Webster, 1612). Cornelia, driven insane by the
wickedness of her children, appears with flowers which
she hands to the bystanders, saying:

[1] Cf. LAERTES. This nothing 's more than matter.
                           (IV. i. 172)
   Note also the verbal echo of Polonius:
     Though this be madness, yet there is method in 't!
                         (II. ii. 206-7)

> You 're very wellcome.
> *There's Rosemarie for you, and Rue for you,*
> Hearts-ease for you. I pray make much of it.
> *I have left more for my selfe.*[1]

(V. iv. 70-3)

This, I think, completes the account of the more conspicuous resemblances to individual characters in *Hamlet*.

---

[1] Cf. OPHELIA. *There's rosemary . . . There's rue for you; and here's some for me.*

(IV. i. 173 ff.)

VI

IMITATIONS OF INDIVIDUAL SCENES FROM *HAMLET*

CERTAIN incidents in *Hamlet* which enjoyed special popularity with the London audiences came
in for their share of imitation, if not open plagiarism.
In the order of occurrence, these incidents may be listed
as: Laertes' farewell to Ophelia; the entrance of the
players, including Hamlet's advice to them; the closet
scene; and finally, the graveyard scene.

When Laertes is about to depart for Paris, being a
true son of old Polonius, he thinks a few moral precepts
appropriate to the occasion. He warns his sister to be
particularly careful of her virtue, and points out the
dangers in her intimacy with the Prince, whose life must
be governed not by his own will but by state policy.
In subsequent plays occur at least four imitations of this
episode, two of which echo Laertes' description of the
snares laid for the virtuous maiden, and the remaining
two, his explanation of the difficulties attendant upon
marriages of state.

The most obvious of these, perhaps, is the passage in
The Fair Maid of the Inn (Beaumont and Fletcher,
1626) in which Cesario addresses his sister Clarissa:

> Interpret not Clarissa, my true zeal
> In giving you counsel, to transcend the bounds
> That should confine a brother; 'tis your honor,

And peace of mind (which honor last will leave you)
I labor to preserve, and though you yet are
Pure and untainted, and resolve to be so:
Having a Fathers eye, and Mothers care
In all your ways to keep you fair, and upright.
In which respects my best advices must
Appear superfluous; yet since love, dear Sister,
Will sometimes tender things unnecessary,
Misconstrue not my purpose . . .
                              Excuse me,
As you would do a Lapidary, whose whole fortunes
Depend upon the safety of one Jewel,
If he think no case precious enough
To keep it in full lustre, nor no locks
Though lending strength to Iron doors sufficient
To guard it, and secure him; you to me are
A Gemm of more esteem, and priz'd higher
Than Usurers do their Muck, or great men Title.

Clarissa assures him:

                              I see brother
The mark you shoot at, and much thank your love;
But for my Virgin Jewel which is brought
In comparison with your Diamond, rest assur'd
It shall not fall in such a workmans hands
Whose ignorance or malice shall have power
To cast one cloud upon it, but still keep
Her native splendor.

He nevertheless warns her to guard her reputation:

Yet let me tell you, (but still with that love,
I wish to increase between us) that *you are
Observ'd* against the gravity long maintain'd

In Italy (*where to see a maid unmasqu'd*
Is held a blemish) *to be over-frequent*
In giving or receiving visits . . .
                                    You are fair,
And *beauty draws temptations on.*[1]

Then, like Ophelia, she suggests that he use some of his own advice:

(*However indulgent to your selves, you brothers*
Allow no part of freedom to your Sisters)
I hope 'twill not pass for a crime in me
To grant access and speech to noble suitors;
And you escape for innocent, that descend
To a thing so far beneath you.
                    (IX, pp. 144-6; cf. *Hamlet*, I. iii. 29 ff.)

Before setting out for Athens, Orgilus, in *The Broken Heart*, asks one last favor from his sister:

Euphranea, thus upon thy cheeks I print
A brother's kiss; more careful of thine honour,
Thy health, and thy well-doing, than my life.
Before we part, in presence of our father,
I must prefer a suit t' ye.

When she affectionately bids him speak, his request, though more exacting than that of Laertes, implies a similar motive:

[1] Cf. LAERTES. The chariest *maid* is prodigal enough
          If she unmask her beauty to the moon.

                                              (I. iii. 36-7)

      POLONIUS. 'Tis told me he *hath very oft of late*
          Given private time to you, and you yourself
          Have of your audience been most free and bounteous.
                                              (I. iii. 91-3)

> Promise
> Never to pass to any man, however
> Worthy, your faith, till, with our father's leave,
> I give free consent . . .
> 　　　　　　　Thou art young and handsome;
> And 'twere injustice,—more, a tyranny—
> Not to advance thy merit: trust me, sister,
> It shall be my first care to see thee match'd
> As may become thy choice and our contents.
> I have your oath.
>
> 　　　　　　　　　　　(I, pp. 220-1)

More like Laertes, Leonidas, in *The Queen of Corinth* (Beaumont and Fletcher, 1617), not only voices his suspicions regarding the intentions of his sister's lover but also reminds her that the Prince is free to marry only the woman of whom the Queen, his mother, approves:

> I know what 'tis you point at,
> The Prince Theanor's love; let not that cheat you;
> *His vows were but meer Courtship; all his service*
> *But practice how to entrap a credulous Lady:*
> Or grant it serious, yet you must remember
> *He's not to love, but where the Queen his Mother*
> *Must give allowance, which to you is barr'd up:*
> And therefore study to forget that ever
> You cherisht such a hope.[1]
>
> 　　　　　　　　　　　(VI, p. 6)

A less obvious resemblance to the solicitous Laertes we observe in Spurio in *The Unfortunate Mother* (Thomas Nabbes, 1639) who advises the Duke of Fer-

[1] Cf. *Hamlet*, I. iii. 16-24. Since Polonius also fears for Ophelia's virtue, his cynical "springes to catch woodcocks" is echoed in Leonidas' warning that the Prince's services are "but practice how to entrap a credulous lady."

rara to remember his position and not to marry Melissa, Spurio's sister, as the Duke desires. Spurio reminds the Duke of the importance to the state of an appropriate marriage:

> Y' are a Prince
> And *every act of yours concernes a state,*
> *Not your meere person onely:* what you doe
> Must therefore deeply be consider'd on . . .
> Princes should wed with Princesse: where there is
> An innate Majesty on both sides, that
> Well mixt, makes up an issue fit for rule,
> And the successive dignities.
>
> (*Old English Plays, New Series,* ed. by A. H. Bullen,
> II, p. 98; cf. *Hamlet,* I. iii. 16-24)

Thomas Middleton's interest in the travelling players of *Hamlet* manifests itself in three comedies: *A Mad World, My Masters* (1606), *The Mayor of Queenborough* (1617-8), and *The Spanish Gypsy* (1623). In *A Mad World, My Masters* Sir Bounteous questions his servant who enters to announce the arrival of the players:

> How now? what news brings thee in stumbling now?

The servant explains his interruption:

> There are certain players come to town, sir, and desire to interlude before your worship.

His master at once consents:

> Players? by the mass, they are welcome; they'll grace my entertainment well. But for certain players, there thou liest, boy; they were never more uncertain in their lives; now up, and now down; they know not when to

play, where to play, nor what to play; not when to
play, for fearful fools; where to play, for puritan fools;
nor what to play, for critical fools.[1]

(V. i. 25-34)

Then he proceeds to greet the actors individually:

And which is your politician amongst you? now
i' faith, he that works out restraints, makes best legs
at court, and has a suit made of purpose for the company's business; which is he? come, be not afraid of
him . . . give me thy hand.

(V. i. 59-65)

Finally he asks the name of the play and learns that it
is *The Slip*. Since the players have planned to rob the
audience, the name of this play-within-a-play, like *The
Mouse-Trap*, designates its purpose.

Similarly, in *The Mayor of Queenborough*, Amin-
adab ushers in a company of actors requesting leave to
perform in the town hall. Asked if they are comedians,
the Second Player replies:

We are, sir; *comedians, tragedians, tragi-comedians,
comi-tragedians, pastorists,* humourists, clownists, satirists: we have them, sir, from the hug to the smile,
from the smile to the laugh, from the laugh to the
handkerchief.[2]

(V. i. 75-8)

[1] Similarly, when Hamlet is informed of the arrival of the players
at Elsinore, he first expresses his pleasure and then comments upon
conditions in the theatre (II. ii. 325 ff.).

[2] Cf. POLONIUS. The best actors in the world, either for *tragedy,
comedy*, history, *pastoral,* pastoral-comical, historical-pastoral, tragical-
historical, tragical-comical-historical-pastoral, scene individable, or
poem unlimited.

(II. ii. 406-10)

In *The Spanish Gypsy*, among the gypsies coming to perform in Madrid is Roderigo, the son of the Corregidor of that city, in disguise. Fernando, his father, who has recognized the youth in spite of his disguise, greets the band and then plunges at once into a discussion of the art of acting:

> There is a way
> Which the Italians and the Frenchmen use,
> That is, on a word given, or some slight plot,
> The actors will extempore fashion out
> Scenes neat and witty.

Alvarez, the leader, assures him that these players have a similar skill, and asks him to suggest a subject. The Corregidor complies, and then adds a part of his own invention to the original in order to force Roderigo to reveal his identity. To that young man, who happens to be the poet of the troupe, Fernando hands the interpolation:

> To save you a labour,
> Look you, against your coming I projected
> This comic passage; your drama, that's the scene . . .
> I lay in our own country, Spain . . .
> Here's a brave part for this old gypsy; look you,
> The father: read the plot; this young she-gypsy,
> The lady: now the son, play him yourself.
>
> (IV. ii. 37-51; cf. *Hamlet*, II. ii. 550-7)

Then the Corregidor, again like Hamlet, advises the actors how the parts should be played:

> Play him up high; not like a pantaloon
> But hotly, nobly, checking this his son,
> Whom make a very rake-hell, debosh'd fellow.
>
> (IV. ii. 65-7; cf. *Hamlet*, III. ii. 1 ff.)

The most detailed imitation of Hamlet's advice to the
players occurs in *The Antipodes* (Richard Brome, 1638)
in Letoy's speech to his fellow-actors just before the
play:

> Trouble not your head with my conceite,
> But minde your part. Let me not see you act now,
> In your Scholasticke way, you brought to towne
>   wi' yee,
> *With see saw sacke a downe, like a Sawyer;*
> *Nor in a Comicke Scene, play Hercules furens,*
> *Tearing your throat to split the Audients eares.*
> And you Sir, you had got a tricke of late,
> Of holding out your bum in a set speech;
> Your fingers fibulating on your breast,
> As if your Buttons, or your Band-strings were
> Helpes to your memory. Let me see you in 't
> No more I charge you. No, nor you sir, in
> That over-action of the legges I told you of,
> Your singles, and your doubles, Look you—thus—
> Like one o' th' dancing Masters o' the Beare-garden;
> And when you have spoke, at end of every speech,
> Not minding the reply, you turne you round
> As Tumblers doe; when betwixt every feat
> They gather wind, by firking up their breeches.
> Ile none of these, absurdities in my house.
> *But words and action married so together,*
> *That shall strike harmony in the eares and eyes*
> *Of the severest, if judicious Criticks.*[1]

---

[1] Cf. HAMLET. Nor *do not saw the air too much with your hand,
thus;* but use all gently: for in the very torrent, tempest, and, as I
may say, whirlwind of passion, you must acquire and beget a tem-
perance that may give it smoothness. *O! it offends me to the soul
to hear a robustious periwig-pated fellow tear a passion to tatters,
to very rags, to split the ears of the groundlings . . . Suit the action*

At this point Quaile-pipe interposes:

> *My lord we are corrected.*[1]

But Letoy ignores him:

> *Goe, be ready:* [*Turning to the Clown.*
> But you Sir are incorrigible, and
> *Take license to your selfe, to adde unto*
> *Your parts, your owne free fancy; and sometimes*
> *To alter, or diminish what the writer*
> *With care and skill compos'd:* and when you are
> To speake to your coactors in the Scene,
> *You hold interloquutions with the Audients.*

Biplay resents this censure:

> That is a way my Lord has bin allow'd
> On elder stages to move mirth and laughter.

Letoy replies:

> Yes in the dayes of Tarlton and Kempe,
> Before the stage was purg'd from barbarisme,
> And brought to the perfection it now shines with.
> Then fooles and jesters spent their wits, because
> The Poets were wise enough to save their owne
> For profitabler uses.[2]

(III, pp. 259-60)

---

to the word, the word to the action; with this special observance,
that you o'erstep not the modesty of nature . . . Now, this over-
done, or come tardy off, though it make the unskilful laugh, *cannot
but make the judicious grieve; the censure of which one must in
your allowance o'erweigh a whole theatre of others.*

(III. ii. 4 ff.)

[1] Cf. FIRST PLAYER. I hope we have reformed that indifferently
with us.

(III. ii. 38-9)

[2] Cf. HAMLET. And *let those that play your clowns speak no
more than is set down for them; for there be of them that will*

Imitations of the closet scene are not confined to such plays as *Antonio's Revenge*,[1] *The Fatal Contract*,[2] and *The Maids Tragedy*,[3] where borrowing is extensive, but may be found unaccompanied by other resemblances to *Hamlet* in *The Revenger's Tragedy* (Cyril Tourneur, 1607), *The Second Part of the Iron Age* (Thomas Heywood, 1613), *The Tragedy of Thierry and Theodoret* (Beaumont and Fletcher, 1617), and, though not so distinct, in one or two other plays.

In *The Revenger's Tragedy*, Vendice and Hippolito threaten their mother Gratiana, who has been bribed by Vendice, in disguise, to sell her own daughter to the dissolute Prince Lusurioso. Gratiana, like Gertrude, first feigns ignorance of her son's charges, then in tears admits her guilt, and at last resolves to live a better life. When Vendice drags her to the stage and begins his arraignment, she, certain that they can know nothing of her shameful bargain, feigns astonishment:

> What mean my sons? *what, will you murder me?*

Vendice exclaims:

> Wicked, unnatural parent!

And Hippolito:

> Fiend of women!

---

themselves laugh to set on some quantity of barren spectators to laugh too, though in the meantime some necessary question of the play be then to be considered. That's villainous, and shows a most pitiful ambition in the fool that uses it. *Go, make you ready.*

(III. ii. 40-7)

[1] See pp. 21-2.
[2] See pp. 44-5.
[3] See pp. 68-71.

She becomes terrified:

> O! are sons turn'd monsters? help! . . . *am not I your mother?*

But Vendice ignores her appeal on that score:

> Thou dost usurp that title now by fraud,
> For in that shell of mother breeds a bawd.[1]

Simulating pious horror, she cries:

> A bawd! O name far loathsomer than hell!

Vendice, however, is not deceived:

> It should be so, knew'st thou thy office well . . .
> Ah! is 't possible? thou only? Powers on high,
> That women should dissemble when they die!

She still refuses to yield:

> Dissemble!

Finally Vendice reveals that he himself had acted as go-between for the Prince in order to test her virtue.

She then breaks down, confesses her sin, and begs forgiveness:

> O sons, forgive me! to myself I 'll prove more true;
> You that should honor me, I kneel to you.

But Vendice does not cease until he is certain that she

---

[1] Cf. QUEEN. *Have you forgot me?*
HAMLET.   No, by the rood, not so.
  You are "the Queen," your husband's brother's wife,
    And—*would it were not so!—you are my mother!* . . .
QUEEN. What wilt thou do? *Thou wilt not murder me?*
(III. iv. 14 ff.)

realizes the vileness of her contemplated act. After she has wept awhile, she penitently exclaims:

> O you Heavens! take *this infectious spot out of my soul,*
> I'll rinse it in seven waters of mine eyes!
> Make my tears salt enough to taste of grace.
> To weep is to our sex naturally given:
> But to weep truly, that's a gift from heaven.[1]
>
> (IV. iv. p. 413 ff.)

In *The Second Part of the Iron Age*, we find a situation even more like that in *Hamlet* in that it involves the appearance of a Ghost. Orestes, determined to avenge the murder of his father, first kills his mother's paramour Egistus, who was her accomplice, and as he watches her weeping over the corpse, exclaims:

> Can you find teares for such an abject Groome,
> That had not for an husband one to shed?
> Oh monstrous, monstrous woman! is this carrion,
> Is this dead Dog, (Dog said I?) nay what's worse,
> Worthy the sigh or mourning of a Queene,
> When a King lies unpittied?

She demands:

> *Thou a sonne?*

Instantly he retorts:

> *The name I am asham'd of:* oh Agamemnon,
> How sacred is thy name and memory!

---

[1] Cf. QUEEN.   O Hamlet, speak no more!
   Thou turn'st mine eyes into *my very soul*;
   And there I see *such black and grained spots*
   As will not leave their tinct.

(III. iv. 88-91)

Whose acts shall fill all forraigne Chronicles
With admiration, and most happy hee
That can with greatest Art but booke thy deeds:
Yet whilst this rottennesse, this gangreen'd flesh
Whose carkas is as odious as his name
Shall stinking lie, able to breede a Pest,
Hee with a Princesse teares to be imbalm'd,
And a King lie neglected?[1]

Next he accuses her of murder, but she denies all guilt, whereupon the Ghost of the murdered man enters. As in the closet scene in *Hamlet*, it is visible only to the son. After greeting this supernatural visitant, Orestes triumphantly turns to his mother:

Lady see.

In astonishment she asks:

See what?

Like Gertrude, she believes her son insane:

Thy former murder *makes thee mad.*

Ignoring her he addresses his father:

Rest Ghost in peace, I now am satisfied,
And neede no further witnesse.

Turning again to her he inquires:

Saw you nothing?

She answers:

What should I see save this sad spectacle,
Which blood-shootes both mine eyes.

[1] Cf. *Hamlet*, III. iv. 14-16, 53-88. Like Hamlet, Orestes expresses regret for his kinship with his adulterous mother and his amazement that she could leave his noble father for her loathsome paramour.

He persists:

> *And nothing else?*

When she reiterates her denial, he tells her:

> Mine eyes are clearer sighted then, and see
> Into thy bosome. Murdresse.[1]

Not in the least deceived by her pretended astonishment at his accusation he rushes on:

> Incestuous strumpet, whose adulteries
> When Treason could not hide, thou thoughtst to cover
> With most inhumane murder.
>
> (III, pp. 421-3)

Heywood's Ghost differs from the Ghost in *Hamlet*, however, in that instead of interceding for the sinful woman, it urges her immediate punishment.

In *The Tragedy of Thierry and Theodoret* the inter-

---

[1] Cf. HAMLET. What would your gracious figure?
QUEEN. *Alas, he's mad!*
HAMLET. Do you not come your tardy son to chide,
    That, laps'd in time and passion, lets go by
    The important acting of your dread command? . . .
QUEEN. To whom do you speak this?
HAMLET.   *Do you see nothing there?*
QUEEN. Nothing at all; *yet all that is I see.*
HAMLET. *Nor did you nothing hear?*
QUEEN.   No; nothing but ourselves . . .
    This is the very coinage of your brain.
    This bodiless creation *ecstasy*
    Is very cunning in.
HAMLET. Ecstasy!
    My pulse, as yours, doth temperately keep time,
    And makes as healthful music. It is not madness
    That I have utter'd.
                    (III. iv. 104 ff.)

view between Gertrude and her son is again copied in
Theodoret's accusation of his wicked mother:

> Witness the daily Libels, almost Ballads . . .
> Are made upon your lust . . .
> > *Now you would blush,*
> *But your black tainted blood dare not appear*
> For fear I should fright that too.

In anger she exclaims:

> O ye gods! . . . *Art thou a son?*

He answers:

> *The more my shame is of so bad a mother,*
> *And more your wretchedness you let me be so.*

Nevertheless he assures her that as soon as she repents
he will honor her as his mother:

> But woman, for a mothers name has left me
> Since you have left your honor; *Mend these ruins,*
> And build again that broken fame, and fairly;
> Your most intemperate fires have burnt . . .
> > And lest Art
> Should loose her self in act, *to call back custome,*
> *Leave these,* and live *like Niobe.* I told you how
> And *when your eyes have dropt away remembrance*
> *Of what you were. I'm your Son!* performe it.[1]
> > (X, pp. 3-4)

---

[1] QUEEN. *Have you forgot me?*
  HAMLET.   No, by the rood, not so.
      You are "the Queen," your husband's brother's wife,
      And—*would it were not so!—you are my mother!* . . .
      O shame! *Where is thy blush?* . . .
                Confess yourself to heaven;
      Repent what's past, avoid what is to come . . .

But in this play repentance does not follow the son's bitter denunciation.

Two other possible imitations of the scene—less pronounced, perhaps, because of the absence of the mother-son relationship—appear in *A Woman is a Weathercock* (Nathaniel Field, 1609) and *The Two Noble Kinsmen*. In Field's play, the faithless Bellafront, seeing her former betrothed Scudmore enter her chamber, realizes his desperation and calls for help. But he refuses to let her escape and reproaches her for her inconstancy. At length she penitently cries:

> O, I am sick of my corruption!
> For God's sake, do not speak a word more to me.

He nevertheless continues all the more vehemently until she again interrupts:

> O, thy dear words have knock'd at my heart's gates,
> And enter'd. They have pluck'd the devil's vizard
> (That did deform this face, and blind my soul)
> Off, and thy Bellafront presents herself,
> Lav'd in a bath of contrite virginal tears.
>   (Dodsley's *Old English Plays* ed. by W. C. Hazlitt,
>   XI, pp. 51-3; cf. *Hamlet*, III. iv. 88-91, 156)

> That monster, *custom, who all sense doth eat,*
> Of habits devil, is angel yet in this,
> That to the use of actions fair and good
> He likewise gives a frock or livery
> That aptly is put on . . .
> *And when you are desirous to be bless'd,*
> *I'll blessing beg of you.*
>
>   (III. iv. 14 ff.)

Also—

> *Like Niobe,* all tears.
>
>   (I. ii. 149)

In *The Two Noble Kinsmen*, Emilia's comparison of the pictures of Palamon and Arcite echoes Hamlet's contrast of his father with his uncle:

> *What an eye!*
> Of what a fiery sparkle, and quick sweetness:
> Has this young Prince! here Love himself sits smiling,
> Just such another wanton Ganimead,
> Set Love a fire with, and enforc'd the god
> Snatch up the goodly Boy, and set him by him
> A shining constellation: *what a brow,*
> Of what a spacious Majesty he carries!
> Arch'd like the great ey'd Juno's, but far sweeter,
> Smoother than Pelops Shoulder . . .
>   Palamon
> Is but his foil, to him, a mere dull shadow,
> He 's swarth, and meagre, of an eye as heavy
> As if he had lost his mother.

> (IX, pp. 351-2; cf. *Hamlet*, III. iv. 53 ff.)

Indubitable imitations of the graveyard scene appear in *The Valiant Welshman* (R. A., 1615) and *The Jealous Lovers* (Thomas Randolph, 1632). In *The Valiant Welshman* (Act IV, Scene iii) a "company of rustickes" enter with the body of Gloster. Prince Caradoc addresses them:

> How now, Sirs,
> What heavy spectacle affronts our eyes?

Ignoring his query, the group sets about preparations for the inquest. The prince tries again:

> Whose body is that, my friends?

The leader of the group, the Clown, then answers:

> Tis not a body, sir, tis but a carkase, sir, *some Gentle-man* it seemes; for *if hee had beene a poore man, that labours for his living, he would have found somewhat else to doe, and not to have hangde himselfe.*

After the Prince withdraws, the Clown begins the inquest:

> My masters, and fellow questmen, this is the point, we are to search out the course of law, *whether this man* that has hangde himself, *be accessary to his own death or no* . . . I put this point to you, whether every one that hangs himselfe, be willing to die or no?

One of his companions declares:

> I, I, sure he is willing.

But the Clown disagrees:

> I say no, for the hangman hangs himselfe, and yet he is not willing to die.

In true vaudeville fashion the question now is asked:

> How dos the hangman hang himselfe?

The conversation continues in the same vein:

> CLOWN. I mary dos he, sir; for if he have not a man to doe his office for him, he must hang himselfe: *ergo,* every man that hangs himselfe is not willing to die.
> FIRST NEIGHBOR. He sayes very true indeed: but now sir, being dead, who shall answere the King for his subject?
> CLOWN. Mary sir, he that hangd his subject.
> SECOND NEIGHBOR. That was himselfe.

THIRD NEIGHBOR. No sir, I doe thinke *it was the halter* that hangde him.

CLOWN. I, in a sort, but *that was, se offendendo,* for it may be, he meant to have broke the halter, and *the halter held him out of his owne defence.*

FIRST NEIGHBOR. But is not the Ropemaker in danger that made it?

CLOWN. No, for hee goes backeward, when tis made, and therefore cannot see before, what will come after; neyther is the halter in fault, for hee might urge the halter, *nolens volens,* (as the learned say) neyther is he in fault, because his time was come that he should be hanged: and therefore I doe conclude, that he was conscious and guiltlesse of his owne death: Moreover, *he was a Lord, and a Lord in his owne precinct has authority to hang and draw* himselfe.[1]

(IV. iii. 1 ff.)

[1] Cf. FIRST CLOWN. How can that be, unless she drowned herself in her own defense?

SECOND CLOWN. Why, 'tis found so.

FIRST CLOWN. It must be *se offendendo*; it cannot be else. For here lies the point: if I drown myself wittingly, it argues an act; and an act hath three branches; it is—to act, to do, and to perform: *argal,* she drowned herself wittingly.

SECOND CLOWN. Nay, but hear you, goodman delver, —

FIRST CLOWN. Give me leave.—Here lies the water; good: here stands the man; good: if the man go to this water, and drown himself, it is, *will-he-nill-he,* he goes—mark you that! but *if the water come to him, and drown him, he drowns not himself: argal,* he that is not guilty of his own death shortens not his own life.

SECOND CLOWN. But is this law?

FIRST CLOWN. Ay, marry, is 't; crowner's quest law.

SECOND CLOWN. Will you ha' the truth on 't? *If this had not been a gentlewoman, she should have been buried out o' Christian burial.*

(V. i. 6-26)

In other words, the Clowns in both plays are considering the problem of Christian burial for a suicide. In *Hamlet*, although they accuse the water of drowning Ophelia, they suspect that the victim's high rank is actually the reason for her burial in consecrated ground. Similarly, in *The Valiant Welshman* they attribute the responsibility for suicide to the "halter that hangde him"; but they, too, seem to feel that his noble title somehow is involved.

The repartee of the sexton in *The Jealous Lovers* echoes first the homely wit of the gravediggers and later the more philosophical irony of Hamlet. Randolph's clown introduces himself to Asotus and his fellow-mourners as—

> The last of tailors, sir, that ne'er take measure of you while you have hope to wear a new suit—

and informs them that he lives "as worms do, by the dead."[1] Asked if any soldiers are buried in the church-yard, he picks up a skull and continues in the style of the Melancholy Dane:

> *This was a captain's skull*, one that carried a storm in his countenance and a tempest in his tongue; the great bugbear of the city, that threw drawers down the stairs as familiarly as quart-pots; and had a pension from the barber-chirurgeons for breaking of pates: a fellow that had ruined the noses of more bawds and panders than the disease belonging to the trade; and yet I remember, when he went to burial, another corse took the wall of him, and the bandog ne'er grumbled.

[1] I, pp. 137-8; cf. *Hamlet*, V. i. 43-61.

Selecting another skull, he tells them:

This was a poetical noddle. O, the sweet lines, choice
language, eloquent figures, besides the jests, half-jests,
quarter-jests, and quibbles that have come out o' these
chaps that yawn so! He has not now so much as a new-
coined compliment to procure him a supper. The best
friend he has may walk by him now, and yet have
ne'er a jeer put upon him. His mistress had a little dog
deceased the other day, and all the wit in this noddle
could not pump out an elegy to bewail it. He has been
my tenant these seven years, and in all that while I
never heard him rail against the times, or complain of
the neglect of learning.

Asked how death treats the ladies, he answers:

This was the prime madam in Thebes, the general mistress, the only adored beauty. Little would you think
there were a couple of ears in these two auger-holes:
or that this pit had been arched over with a handsome
nose, that had been at the charges to maintain half a
dozen of several silver arches to, uphold the bridge.
*It had been a mighty favour once to have kissed these
lips that grin so.* This mouth out of all the madam's
boxes cannot now be furnished with a set of teeth.
She was the coyest, [most] overcurious dame in all
the city: her chambermaid's misplacing of a hair was
as much as her place came to. *O, if that lady now
could but behold this physnomy of hers in a looking-
glass, what a monster would she imagine herself!*
Will all her perukes, tires, and dresses; with her
chargeable teeth, with her ceruse and pomatum, and
the benefit of her painter and doctor, make this idol up
again?

> *Paint, ladies, while you live, and plaister fair;*
> *But when the house is fallen, 'tis past repair.*[1]

Finally, for his views on the futility of a lawyer's life he borrows Hamlet's very words:

> Look here! *this is a lawyer's skull.* There was a tongue in 't once, a damnable eloquent tongue, that would almost have persuaded any man to the gallows. This was a turbulent, busy fellow, till death gave him his *quietus est.* And yet I ventured to rob him of his gown and the rest of his habiliments, to the very buckram bag . . . [*To the skull.*] *Now a man may clap you o' th' coxcomb with his spade, and never stand in fear of an action of battery.*[2]

> (I, pp. 139-44)

In each instance, as in *Hamlet*, the contrast is made between the former pride of the individual and his present humble state.

In a similar melancholy vein are Vendice's two soliloquies in *The Revenger's Tragedy*, in both of which, as

---

[1] Cf. HAMLET. *Here hung those lips that I have kissed I know not how oft.* Where be your gibes now? your gambols? your songs? your flashes of merriment that were wont to set the table on a roar? Not one now, *to mock your own grinning?* quite chapfallen? *Now get you to my lady's chamber, and tell her, let her paint an inch thick, to this favour she must come. Make her laugh at that!*

> (V. i. 196-204)

[2] Cf. HAMLET. Why might not that be *the skull of a lawyer?* Where be his quiddities now? his quillets, his cases, his tenures, and his tricks? *Why does he suffer this rude knave now to knock him about the sconce with a dirty shovel, and will not tell him of his action of battery?*

> (V. i. 101-6)

Cf. also *Hamlet*, III. i. 75.

he gazes on the skull of his "poisoned love," he medi-
tates on the transitoriness of feminine beauty:

> When two heaven-pointed diamonds were set
> In those unsightly rings—then 'twas a face
> So far beyond the artificial shine
> Of any woman's bought complexion,
> That the uprightest man (if such there be,
> That sin but seven times a day) broke custom,
> And made up eight with looking after her.
>
> (I. i. p. 344)

> Here 's an eye,
> Able to tempt a great man—to serve God:
> *A pretty hanging lip*, that has forgot now to dissemble.
> Methinks this mouth should make a swearer tremble . . .
> *Does every proud and self-affecting dame*
> *Camphire her face for this*, and grieve her Maker
> In sinful baths of milk, when many an infant starves
> For her superfluous outside—all for this?
> Who now bids twenty pounds a night? prepares
> Music, perfumes, and sweetmeats? All are hush'd.
> Thou may'st lie chaste now!
>
> (III. iv. pp. 391-2; cf. *Hamlet*, V. i. 196-203)

Other echoes of particular scenes in *Hamlet*, which
are unaccompanied by similarity in action, have been
placed with the allusions.[1]

---

[1] For example, the swearing episode in *The Woman's Prize, or
the Tamer Tam'd* (Beaumont and Fletcher, 1604) which Mr. Munro
(*op. cit.*, I, p. xl) considers an imitation of scene.

VII

BURLESQUES OF *HAMLET*

WHILE *Hamlet* was enjoying its greatest popularity, immediately after Shakespeare's triumphant revision, it was occasionally made the subject of
satire, or, as Dr. Thorndike puts it, "a little pleasant
burlesque,"[1] and characters, scenes, or lines that spe-
cially impressed the audience were parodied then much
as they have been ever since.[2] The majority of these
parodies come from two plays entirely by John Marston
and a third which bears the names of Marston, Chapman,
and Jonson; the remainder, from an early play by Beaumont and Fletcher.

In *What You Will* (1601) Marston burlesques the
first entrance of Hamlet after he has assumed the rôle
of madman. Philus, servant to Jacomo, runs upon the
stage, crying:

O, I beseech you, sir, reclaim his wits;
My master's *mad, stark mad, alas! for love.*

And a little further in the same scene is the stage
direction—

Enter Jacomo, *unbraced, and carelessly dressed.*

[1] *Op cit.,* p. 203 n.
[2] The poetry of W. S. Gilbert, for instance, is full of witty
parodies of *Hamlet* and other Shakespearean plays.

Philus then comments:

> *Look, where he comes.*[1]

(I. i. 1 ff.)

In *The Malcontent* (1604), also by Marston, appear four more travesties, which are little more than verbal echoes. First, Mendoza's eulogy of women:

> Sweet women! most sweet ladies! nay, angels! . . . O paradise! how majestical is your austerer presence! how imperiously chaste is your more modest face! . . . in body how delicate, in soul how witty, in discourse how pregnant, in life how wary, in favours how judicious, in day how sociable, and in night how—O pleasure unutterable![2]

(I. i. 339 ff.)

Secondly, Aurelia's remark as the eulogist "enters *reading* a sonnet"—

---

[1] Cf. OPHELIA. Lord Hamlet, *with his doublet all unbrac'd,*
   No hat upon his head, his stockings foul'd,
   Ungarter'd, and down-gyved to his ankle,
   Pale as his shirt, his knees knocking each other,
   And with a look so piteous in purport
   As if he had been loosed out of hell
   To speak of horrors, he comes before me.
POLONIUS. *Mad for thy love?*

(II. i. 78-85)

QUEEN. But *look, where* sadly *the poor wretch comes* reading:
       [*Enter* Hamlet, *reading on a book.*

(II. ii. 168)

[2] Cf. HAMLET. What a piece of work is a man! How noble in reason! how infinite in faculty! in form, in moving, how express and admirable! in action how like an angel! in apprehension how like a god! the beauty of the world! the paragon of animals!

(II. ii. 310-5)

Look where the base *wretch comes—*

(I. ii. 66-7)

may point satirically at Gertrude's—

But *look, where* sadly the poor *wretch comes reading—*
(II. ii. 168)

which in turn precedes the stage direction—

Enter Hamlet, *reading on a book.*

Thirdly, Maquerelle's retort to Fernese, whose vows are truly "mere implorators of unholy suits"—

Believe him not; traps to catch pole-cats—

(V. iii. 147-8)

burlesques Polonius' warning to his daughter—

Ay, springes to catch woodcocks.

(I. iii. 115)

Finally, Malevole's sarcastic admonition to Bilioso of the dangers threatening his wife at Court—

Elder of Israel, thou honest defect of wicked nature and obstinate ignorance, when did thy wife let thee lie with her—

(III. i. 172-4)

points at Hamlet's veiled reply to Polonius, intended to inform him of the perils in the King's attentions to Ophelia—

O Jephthah, *judge of Israel,* what a treasure hadst thou.
(II. ii. 413-4)

Each passage obtains its comic effect only through its relation to *Hamlet,* and therefore implies an intimate acquaintance with that play on the part of the audience.

In *Eastward Hoe* (1605), in which Marston collaborated with Chapman and Jonson, Hamlet, a footman, rushes to the stage exclaiming:

> What, coachman—my lady's coach! for shame! her ladyship 's ready to come down!
>
> (III. ii. 4-5)

And Potkin, a tankard-bearer, asks:

> 'Sfoot! Hamlet, *are you mad*?
>
> (III. ii. 6)

A few moments later, Gertrude, "her ladyship" to whom Hamlet refers, enters and demands:

> *My coach,* for the love of heaven, *my coach!*
> In good truth, I shall swoon else.
>
> (III. ii. 28-9)

Apparently Gertrude is mimicking Ophelia's—

> Come, *my coach*—
>
> (IV. i. 72)

for she then sings:

> *His head as white as milk, all flaxen was his hair;*
> *But now he is dead, and laid in his bed,*
> *And never will come again,*

followed by—

> *God be at your labour!*[1]
>
> (III. ii. 79-82)

[1] Obviously a parody of Ophelia's song, especially the lines:
> No, no, *he is dead!*
> *Go to thy death-bed,*
> *He never will come again!*
> His beard was *as white as* snow,
> *All flaxen was his poll.*
>
> (IV. i. 190-4)

Ophelia, like Gertude, concludes with a blessing—
> *God be wi' ye!*

In this same play Hamlet's sarcastic explanation for his mother's hasty marriage—

> Thrift, thrift, Horatio! *the funeral bak'd meats*
> *Did coldly furnish forth the marriage tables—*
>
> (I. ii. 180-1)

is twice echoed in order to lend an amusing touch to Golding's strategic marriage to Gertrude's sister. Touchstone suggests that as a proof of his good-will he should give his son-in-law as fine a marriage feast as Gertrude had, but the frugal Golding replies:

> Let me beseech you, no sir; *the superfluity and cold meat left at their nuptials will with bounty furnish ours.*
>
> (II. i. 164-6)

Later, when Gertrude inquires why her sister is not attending her, Quicksilver discloses the true state of affairs:

> Marry, madam, she's married by this time to prentice Golding. Your father, and some one more, stole to church with 'hem in all the haste, that *the cold meat left at your wedding might serve to furnish their nuptial table.*
>
> (III. ii. 59-63)

Finally, the Queen's description of Ophelia's death—

> Her clothes spread wide,
> *And, mermaid-like, awhile they bore her up—*
>
> (IV. iii. 174-5)

is parodied in *Eastward Hoe* by Slitgut, who thus describes the shipwreck as seen from the Isle of Gulls:

Ay me! see another remnant of this unfortunate shipwreck, or some other. A woman, i' faith, a woman;
though it be almost at St. Katherine's, I discern it to
be a woman, for all her body is above the water, and
her clothes swim about her most handsomely. O, *they
bear her up most bravely!* has not a woman reason to
love the taking up of her clothes the better while she
lives, for this? Alas! how busy the rude Thames is
about her! a pox o' that wave! it will drown her,
i' faith, 'twill drown her! Cry God mercy, she has
'scaped it—I thank heaven she has 'scaped it! O how she
swims *like a mermaid*!

(IV. i. 60-71)

The Woman-Hater (Beaumont and Fletcher, 1606)
also burlesques lines which mark particularly exciting
moments in *Hamlet* and were therefore familiar to the
audience. The parody of the Ghost's first admonition
to his son lends absurdity to the Count's conversation
with the greedy Lazarello:

COUNT. Lazarello, bestirr thy self nimbly and sodainly,
  and hear me with patience [to hear].
LAZARELLO. Let me not fall from my self; *Speak I 'm
  bound.*
COUNT. *So art thou to revenge, when thou shalt hear*
  the fish head is gone, and we know not whither.[1]

(X, pp. 92-3)

On another occasion, when Lazarello is asked his age,
he replies:

---

[1] Cf. GHOST. Pity me not, *but lend thy serious hearing*
        To what I shall unfold.
  HAMLET.   *Speak; I am bound to hear.*
  GHOST. *So art thou to revenge, when thou shalt hear!*
                                              (I. v. 5-8)

> *Full eight and twenty several Almanacks*
> Have been compiled, all for several years
> Since first I drew this breath, four prentiships
> Have I most truely served in this world:
> *And eight and twenty times hath Phoebus Car*
> *Run out his yearly course since.*

One of the bystanders comments:

> How like an ignorant Poet he talks.[1]

(X, p. 90)

Any burlesque depends for its effect upon the familiarity of the audience with the object ridiculed. Since this early play of Beaumont and Fletcher, as well as *The Malcontent* and *What You Will* by Marston, and *Eastward Hoe* in which he collaborated, all appeared shortly after *Hamlet*, we are assured of the immediate popularity of Shakespeare's play. Nor should we fail to note that Marston's humorous allusions in these comedies reflect quite as clearly as his more serious borrowings in *Antonio's Revenge* the strong influence of *Hamlet*, which began soon after the composition of *Antonio and Mellida*.

[1] Cf. PLAYER KING. *Full thirty times hath Phoebus' cart* gone round
   Neptune's salt wash and Tellus' orbed ground,
   And thirty dozen moons with borrow'd sheen
   About the world have times twelve thirties been.

(III. ii. 159-62)

VIII

ALLUSIONS TO *HAMLET*

IN ADDITION to the evidence already adduced, the plays from 1600 to 1642 afford almost five hundred allusions—occasionally only paraphrases but more often actual verbal echoes—to lines in *Hamlet*. Some of them are of little importance when considered apart from the imitations already discussed; others might be regarded as faint memories on the part of Shakespeare's contemporaries. Yet, taken as a whole, they disclose as nothing else could the deep impression *Hamlet* made upon the age.

The plays containing these allusions have been assembled according to date, which only too often for lack of sufficient information must be based on conjecture.[1] For the sake of convenience in discussion the period may be divided into two parts—the first, 1600 to 1613, when Shakespeare was engaged in dramatic activity; and the second, 1614 to 1642, from his retirement to the closing of the theatres. Before 1614 the number of plays each year containing allusions to *Hamlet* was decidedly larger than afterward; indeed, in each of six of the fourteen years at the beginning of the century—1602, 1604, 1606, 1608, 1610, and 1613—there appeared

---

[1] For the dates of these plays I have consulted Sir E. K. Chambers, *The Elizabethan Stage* (1923), Alfred Harbage, *Cavalier Drama* (1936), F. E. Schelling, *Elizabethan Drama* (1908), and *The Cambridge History of English Literature* (1910). Wherever a difference of opinion occurs, the most recent authority is used.

at least five such plays. After 1614, however, in only three years—1626, 1632, and 1638—were there as many as five plays with allusions.

The following table records the number of allusions before 1642 to each scene in *Hamlet* (a total of 474):[1]

I					II		III								IV			V	
i	ii	iii	iv	v	i	ii	i	ii	iii	iv	v	vi	vii	viii	i	ii	iii	i	ii
20	40	13	9	66	3	73	39	51	34	38	0	1	3	10	20	0	8	31	15

As previously stated,[2] a comparison of the finished version of *Hamlet* with the hypothetical *Ur-Hamlet* as we know it through the First Quarto, the *Fratricide Punished*, and the prose accounts, reveals Shakespeare's responsibility for the transformation of the Ghost, for the philosophical treatment of the hero, for the introduction of the love-romance, and for the sympathetic portrayal of the repentant Queen. It is interesting, therefore, to observe that the scenes most frequently alluded to are those which contain these contributions by Shakespeare to the play.

The principal ghost scene is, of course, Act I, Scene v; and of 107 allusions to *Hamlet* between 1600 and 1606 (the date of *The Atheist's Tragedy*, the last of the "replies" to *Hamlet*) nineteen, or almost twenty per cent, were directed toward this scene alone. The revival of interest in the tragedy of revenge, of which the ghost is an important feature, may account for these early borrowings, which incidentally seem to corroborate the opinion that Shakespeare began his revision with the

[1] Here as elsewhere in this study the division of acts and scenes adopted by Dr. Joseph Q. Adams in his edition of the tragedy has been followed.

[2] See pp. 10-11.

Ghost.[1] The scene retained its attraction for contemporary playwrights until the closing of the theatres. Lines particularly effective on the stage frequently recurred; for example, the Ghost's "I could a tale unfold," and Hamlet's "O my prophetic soul." Furthermore, the presence of the Ghost in Act I, Scene i, and Act III, Scene iv, was responsible for a large part of the allusions to these two scenes. Yet the dialogue between Hamlet and his mother in the closet scene, the several imitations of which have already been pointed out, inspired its share of allusions.

Hamlet's philosophical attitude toward life is revealed in his soliloquies, in his conversations with Horatio and with Rosencrantz and Guildenstern, in his jibes at old Polonius, and finally, in his meditations in the graveyard. In the early years the passages containing the subtler ideas were ignored, whereas the two soliloquies—the second, "O what a rogue and peasant slave am I" (II. ii. 564 ff.) which permits of much histrionic fervor, and the fourth, the murderous " 'Tis now the very witching time of night" (III. ii. 398 ff.)—were frequently imitated. The allusions to the terrible fifth soliloquy, "Now might I do it pat" (III. iii. 73 ff.), started in 1607 and continued throughout the period. Later the more philosophical soliloquies—the first, "O that this too, too solid flesh would melt" (I. ii. 129 ff.), and the third, "To be, or not to be" (III. i. 56 ff.)—gained in popularity.

Hamlet's outburst of idealism as he talks with his two false friends, beginning "What a piece of work is a man" (II. ii. 310 ff.), was echoed by idealists of later plays.

[1] See pp. 8-9.

His sarcastic replies to Polonius (II. ii. 174 ff.; III. ii. 385 ff.) as well as his ironical comment to Horatio on his mother's hasty marriage, "The funeral bak'd meats . . ." (I. ii. 180-1), both tinged with cynicism and melancholia, were often repeated and paraphrased.

Toward the episode in Hamlet's love affair with Ophelia commonly known as the nunnery scene were directed most of the allusions to Act III, Scene i, not pointed at the third soliloquy. Similarly in Act V, Scene i, the conclusion of the romance, the incident at Ophelia's grave, as well as Hamlet's meditations in the graveyard, inspired frequent imitation. The verbal borrowings thus indicate that *Hamlet* as a reflection of Shakespeare's genius, rather than as a representative of the traditional tragedy of revenge, captivated the interest of contemporary playwrights.

If, then, we concede that it is the Shakespearean element in this tragedy that attracted these writers, we should next consider the men most affected by Shakespeare's genius. Repeatedly drawing on *Hamlet* were Marston, Chettle, Tourneur, and Beaumont and Fletcher. Marston alone was responsible for the entire twenty-six allusions recorded for the year 1601, of which eighteen come from *Antonio's Revenge* and the remaining eight from *What You Will*. Of the twenty-eight allusions in 1604, the same playwright is credited with fourteen. In *Eastward Hoe*, in which Marston collaborated, appear six of the ten allusions recorded for the year 1605. Then, although only two of the twenty-one allusions made in 1606 are found in his comedy *The Dutch Courtesan*, no less than fifteen of a total of twenty-seven occurring in 1610 are taken from his *Insatiate Countess*. Accordingly, were we to omit from our tabulations *Antonio's Revenge*, believed by some scholars to precede *Hamlet*, we still should have forty-five allusions from Marston's pen. Indeed, we shall not find one of his later plays which does not contain a borrowing from *Hamlet*. May we not, therefore, regard this tendency to imitate as evidence of his deep admiration for Shakespeare's play, which—considering the numerous similarities in *Antonio's Revenge*—may explain why Marston changed his original plan for the sequel to *Antonio and Mellida* from a comedy to a tragedy of revenge?

As we might expect, the revenge-plays of Chettle and Tourneur also contain several echoes of *Hamlet*. Of the fourteen allusions recorded for the year 1602, nine are found in *Hoffman*. *The Atheist's Tragedy* contains nine of the twenty-one from plays written in 1606. The presence of these verbal imitations in tragedies which differ in varying degrees from *Hamlet* in their treatment of revenge strengthens the suspicion that contemporary playwrights felt called upon to reply to Shakespeare.

Beginning in 1604 with an imitation in *The Woman's Prize, or the Tamer Tam'd* of the episode in the principal ghost scene in which Hamlet swears Horatio and Marcellus to secrecy (I. v. 145 ff.), Beaumont and Fletcher started a series of borrowings that did not end until 1626, the date assigned to *The Fair Maid of the Inn* and *The Noble Gentleman*, the last plays in which Fletcher is supposed to have collaborated. Of twenty-one verbal echoes recorded for 1606, six come from *The Woman-Hater*. These earlier allusions were somewhat satirical in tone, but more serious borrowing begins in 1608, when nine of a total of seventeen echoes of *Hamlet*

occurred in plays by the two collaborators—eight in
Four Plays or Moral Representations in One, the extensive imitation in which has already been discussed,[1]
and the ninth in *Wit at Several Weapons*. Again in 1610
they were responsible for nine of the total twenty-seven
allusions, seven of which may be found in *Philaster*
alone. *The Maids Tragedy* claims eleven of the sixteen
occurring in 1611. Finally, in 1613, seven of the seventeen are found in plays by these playwrights.

The majority of the allusions after 1614 appear in
the plays of Ford, Heminge, Randolph, and Suckling.
Between Ford and Heminge are divided twenty-eight
of the twenty-nine allusions recorded for 1628—thirteen
in *The Lover's Melancholy* and fifteen in *The Jewes
Tragedy*.[2] In a second play by Heminge, *The Fatal
Contract*, appear sixty-seven of the entire seventy-two
made in 1630. The borrowing in this play obviously ex-
ceeds that in any other; indeed, it is the only play from
which we have to print almost a whole scene in order to
record the verbal echoes alone.[3] In *The Jealous Lovers*,
which contains an imitation of the graveyard scene, we
find nine of the twenty allusions noted for 1632. Finally,
from Suckling's two plays, *Aglaura* and *The Sad One*,
come the fifteen allusions for the year 1637.

The touchstone we have applied thus reveals that
Shakespeare's influence over his contemporaries was far
more powerful than has hitherto been believed. In the
first place, Mr. Munro's allusions to *Hamlet* alone have
been increased tenfold. This remarkable borrowing

[1] See pp. 53-6.
[2] See pp. 193-6.
[3] See pp. 199-200.

shows beyond doubt that contemporary writers recognized the merits of the play and sought to imitate it in their own work. Its extensive influence on the plays of Beaumont and Fletcher, which Mr. Munro calls the principal models in the drama before 1642,[1] further attests to its high reputation in the early part of the seventeenth century. Evidently if Shakespeare's companions did not consider him "the great heir of universal fame," as Mr. Munro maintains, at least they recognized in him a talented dramatist able to make plays that would appeal to the theatre-goers of the day. Most important of all, in my opinion, is the discovery of the relation of *Hamlet* to contemporary tragedies of revenge, for, notwithstanding the authority of Dr. Thorndike and Mr. Munro to the contrary, it seems fairly apparent to me that Shakespeare was responsible for the revival of interest in the revenge-play at the beginning of the century.

[1] See p. 5.

PART TWO

ALLUSIONS TO *HAMLET* FROM 1600 TO 1642

ALLUSIONS TO *HAMLET* FROM 1600 TO 1642

THE following allusions consist of passages, each containing what seems either a verbal echo or a paraphrase of a corresponding passage in *Hamlet*. For the convenience of the reader italics have been used wherever possible in order to indicate the resemblance. Intending that this section be a unit in itself, I have included all passages which, because of their association with plot or with characterization, have appeared elsewhere in preceding chapters. Where such duplication occurs, the reader is referred by means of a footnote to the page where the allusion previously appears. As far as possible, all proverbial expressions and commonplaces have been eliminated. For this reason four of Mr. Munro's forty-five allusions to *Hamlet* have been rejected.[1] All phraseology common to the tragedy of

[1] The four rejected allusions are as follows:

> *Revenge For Honour* (George Chapman?, 1640)
> Makes them run forth like lapwings
> From their warm nest, part of the shell yet sticking
> Unto their downy heads.
>> (II. i. 31-3; cf. *Hamlet*, V. ii. 188-9)

> *The Great Duke of Florence* (Philip Massinger, 1627)
> This exercise hath put you into a sweat;
> Take this and dry it.
>> (II, p. 480; cf. *Hamlet*, V. ii. 293)

> *A Mad World, My Masters* (Thomas Middleton, 1606)
> Shield me you ministers of faith and grace!
>> (IV. i. 34; cf. *Hamlet*, I. iv. 39)

> *Lingua* (Anonymous, 1603)
> The blushing childhood of the cheerful morn

revenge has also been omitted, except when accompanied by further similarity, either in character or context, to *Hamlet*. In spite of the pains thus taken to include only unmistakable verbal imitations, the reader may object to some or desire to add others. Obviously a collection such as this must to a great extent depend upon the compiler's judgment, which, of course, is subject to error.

The allusions are arranged, first, according to the date of the appearance of the play from which they are taken; secondly, alphabetically by playwrights (and if two or more plays by the same playwright appear in any one year, alphabetically according to the title of the play); and finally, if several allusions occur in one play, according to the sequence of the lines alluded to in *Hamlet* (excepting only those few passages containing several allusions the effect of which would be destroyed by rearrangement).

1600

ANONYMOUS

The Distracted Emperor

Thy threats to me are like the kyngs̄ desyer,
As *uneffectuall as the gloawormes fyer.*
> (*Old English Plays* ed. by A. H. Bullen, III, p. 170;
> cf. *Hamlet*, I. v. 90)

> Is almost grown a youth, and overclimbs
> Yonder gilt eastern hills.
> > (Dodsley's *Old English Plays* ed. by W. C. Hazlitt,
> > IX, p. 346; cf. *Hamlet*, I. i. 166-7)

And though in *pollycie* I will not leave
Your lordshypps servyce, yet if *polycie*
Or *brayne* of man may studdye a revendge,
Thys wytt of myne thats seldome showne in vayne
Shall fashyon out a rare one.
> (*Ibid.*, III, p. 183; cf. *Hamlet*, II. ii. 46-8)

Full twoe and twentye severall liverye coatts,
Made & composed all for severall yeares,
Have I runne throughe in your most faythfull service.
> (*Ibid.*, III, p. 182; cf. *Hamlet*, III. ii. 159)

1601

John Marston

Antonio's Revenge

Why, mother, is 't not wondrous strange
I am not mad—I run not frantic, ha?
Knowing, *my father's trunk scarce cold, your love*
Is sought by him that doth pursue my life![1]
> (II. ii. 151-4; cf. *Hamlet*, I. ii. 147-51)

ANTONIO. The other ghost *assum'd my father's shape:*
  Both cried, "*Revenge!*" . . .
  My *jellied blood 's* not thaw'd.
> (I. ii. 111 ff.; cf. *Hamlet*, I. ii. 204-5, 243,
> also I. v. 25)

ANTONIO. Hath the Duke supp'd?
ALBERTO. Yes, and triumphant revels mount aloft.
  The Duke *drinks deep* to overflow his grief.
> (V. i. 21-3; cf. *Hamlet*, I. iv. 7-12)

[1] See p. 20.

Would'st have me cry, run raving up and down,
For my son's loss? Would'st have me turn rank mad,
Or *wring my face with mimic action*;
Stamp, *curse, weep, rage*, and then my bosom strike?
Away, 'tis aspish action, *player-like*.
(I. ii. 314-8; cf. Hamlet, II. ii. 565-71)

Madam, I will not swell, *like a tragedian,*
In forcèd passion of affected strains.
(II. ii. 109-10; cf. Hamlet, II. ii. 565-71)

ANTONIO [*Reading from* Seneca.] Pish, *thy mother was not*
lately widowèd,
    Thy dear affièd love lately defam'd
    With blemish of foul lust, when thou wrotest thus;
    Thou wrapt in furs, beaking thy limbs 'fore fires;
    Forbid'st the frozen zone to shudder. Ha, ha! 'tis nought
    But foamy bubbling of a fleamy brain,
    Nought else but smoke. *O what dank marish spirit,*
    But would be fired with impatience
    At my—
    No more, no more.
(II. ii. 49-58; cf. Hamlet, II. ii. 574-84)

He was the *very hope* of Italy.
(I. ii. 304; cf. Hamlet, III. i. 157)

ALBERTO. Indeed, he's hoarse; the poor boy's voice is
    crack'd.
PANDULPHO. Why, coz! why should it not be hoarse and
    crack'd,
    When *all the strings of nature's symphony*
    Are crack'd and jar?
(IV. ii. 90-3; cf. Hamlet, III. i. 163)

Re-enter Strotzo with Maria, Nutriche, and Lucio. Piero
passeth through his guard, and *talks with Maria with seem-*
ing amourousness; she seemeth to reject his suit, flies to
the tomb, kneels, and kisseth it. Piero bribes Nutriche
and Lucio; they go to her, *seeming to solicit his suit. She*
riseth, offers to go out; Piero stayeth her, tears open his
breast, embraceth and kisseth her; and so they go all out in
state.

(III. i; cf. Hamlet, III. ii)

> *'Tis yet dead night,* yet all the earth is clutch'd
> In the dull leaden hand of snoring sleep;
> No breath disturbs the quiet of the air,
> No spirit moves upon the breast of earth,
> Save howling dogs, night-crows, and screeching owls,
> *Save meagre ghosts,* Piero, and *black thoughts.*
> (I. i. 3-8; cf. Hamlet, III. ii. 397-402)

> *Now gapes the graves,* and through their yawns let loose
> Imprison'd spirits to revisit earth;
> And now, swart night, to swell thy hour out,
> Behold I spurt warm blood in thy black eyes . . .
> Lo thus I heave my blood-dyed hands to heaven,
> Even like *insatiate hell* still crying, More!
> *My heart hath thirsting dropsies after gore.*
> Sound peace and rest to *church, night-ghosts,* and
>   *graves:*
> *Blood cries for blood,* and murder murder craves.
> (III. i. 188 ff.; cf. Hamlet, III. ii. 397-402)

> Ay, I will murder: *graves and ghosts*
> Fright me no more, *I'll suck red vengeance*
> Out of Piero's wounds, Piero's wounds!
> (III. i. 125-7; cf. Hamlet, III. ii. 400-2)

PANDULPHO. And shall yon blood-hound live?
ANTONIO. Have I an *arm*, a *heart*, a *sword*, a *soul*?
>   (IV. ii. 82-3; cf. *Hamlet*, III. viii. 45)

> My father dead: my love attaint of lust . . .
> What, whom, whither, which shall I first lament?
> *A dead father, a dishonour'd wife?*[1]
>   (I. ii. 264 ff.; cf. *Hamlet*, III. viii. 57)

MARIA. [*Of* Mellida.] O piteous end of love! O too, too rude
    hand
Of unrespective death! *Alas, sweet maid!*
>   (IV. i. 284-5; cf. *Hamlet*, V. i. 252-5)

PANDULPHO. I am the miserablest soul that breathes.
ANTONIO. 'Slid, sir, ye lie! by the heart of grief, thou liest!
    I scorn'd that any wretched should survive,
    Outmounting me in that superlative,
    Most miserable, most unmatch'd in woe.
    Who dare assume that but Antonio?
>   (IV. ii. 76-81; cf. *Hamlet*, V. i. 264-80)

What You Will

PHILUS. O, I beseech you, sir, reclaim his wits;
    My master's *mad, stark mad, alas! for love* . . .
    [*Enter* Jacomo, *unbraced, and carelessly dressed.*
    Look, where he comes.[2]
>   (I. i. 1 ff.; cf. *Hamlet*, II. i. 78-85, also
>   II. ii. 168)

>   All that exists,
> Takes valuation from opinion.
>   (I. i. 18-19; cf. *Hamlet*, II. ii. 251-2)

[1] See p. 19.
[2] See pp. 116-17.

Is 't *comedy*, *tragedy*, *pastoral*, moral, nocturnal, or *history?*

> (Induction, l. 90; cf. *Hamlet*, II. ii. 406-10)

LAMPATHO. I'll be reveng'd.
QUADRATUS. How, prithee? *in a play?*

> (IV. i. 172-3; cf. *Hamlet*, II. ii. 621-2)

'Tis just three months.
Shall I speak like a poet?—*thrice hath the horned moon.*[1]

> (III. ii. 17-18; cf. *Hamlet*, III. ii. 161-2)

O Celia! How oft,
When thou hast laid thy cheek upon my breast,
And with lascivious petulancy sued
For hymeneal dalliance, marriage-rites;—
O then, how oft, with passionate protests
And zealous vows, hast thou obliged thy love,
In *dateless bands*, unto Albano's breast!
Then, *did I but mention second marriage,*
With what a bitter hate would she inveigh
'Gainst retail'd wedlocks! "O!" would she lisp,
"*If you should die*,"—then would she slide a tear,
And with a wanton languishment intwist
Her hands,—"*O God, and you should die! Marry?*
Could I love life, my dear Albano dead?
Should any prince possess his widow's bed?"
And now, see, see, I am but rumour'd drown'd.[2]

> (III. ii. 19-34; cf. *Hamlet*, III. ii. 163 ff.)

Now, by *the front of Jove.*

> (IV. i. 210; cf. *Hamlet*, III. iv. 56)

[1] See p. 80.
[2] See pp. 80-1.

1602

Henry Chettle

Hoffman

> Be but appeas'd, sweete hearse
> The dead remembrance of my living father
> And with a hart as iron, *swift as thought*
> I 'le execute justly in such a cause
> Where truth leadeth.[1]

(ll. 5-9; cf. *Hamlet*, I. v. 29-31)

> Therefore without protraction, [sighing], or excuses
> *Sweare to be true*, to ayd [assist] me, *not to stirre*
> *Or contradict me in any enterprise*
> *I shall now undertake, or heare after.*[2]

(ll. 71-4; cf. *Hamlet*, I. v. 169-81)

> What can fortune doe
> That may divert my *traine of pollicy*.[3]

(ll. 1561-2; cf. *Hamlet*, II. ii. 47)

> The *goodliest frame* that ever nature built.

(l. 870; cf. *Hamlet*, II. ii. 305)

> The rarest *peece* of natures *workmanship*.

(l. 960; cf. *Hamlet*, II. ii. 310-1)

> *My true love is not dead,*
> Noe y' are deceivd in him, *my father is.*[4]

(ll. 1343-4; cf. *Hamlet*, IV. i. 23-40)

[1] See p. 24.
[2] See p. 24.
[3] Although the standard editions of *Hamlet* print this phrase as *trail of policy*, it appears in the First Quarto as *traine of policie* (Variorum ed., vol. II, p. 54, l. 724).
[4] See p. 25.

Pray [ye] tell me true,
Could you be patient, or you, or you, or you,
To loose a father and a husband too?[1]

(ll. 1355-7; cf. *Hamlet*, IV. i. 68-70)

Good night good gentlefolkes, brother your hand,
And yours good father, you are my father now . . .
Soe now god-buye, [*soe*] *now god-night indeede*.[2]

(ll. 1397 ff.; cf. *Hamlet*, IV. i. 72-3)

Here, looke, looke here, here is a way goes downe,
Downe, downe a downe, hey downe, downe.
I sung that song, while Lodowicke slept with me.[3]

(ll. 1839-41; cf. *Hamlet*, IV. i. 169-71)

Thomas Dekker

Satiromastix

My name's *Hamlet revenge*![4]

(I, p. 229; cf. *Hamlet*, I. v. 22-5)

The Famous History of Sir Thomas Wyatt

O propheticke soule.

(III, p. 87; cf. *Hamlet*, I. v. 40)

Thomas Heywood

The Royall King, and the Loyall Subject

When I forget thee, may *my operant parts*
Each one forget their office.

(VI, p. 6; cf. *Hamlet*, III. ii. 178)

[1] See p. 25.
[2] See p. 26.
[3] See p. 26.
[4] See p. 37.

Anonymous

How a Man May Choose a Good Wife from a Bad

That is no wrong, which we impute no wrong!
      (Dodsley's *Old English Plays* ed. by W. C. Hazlitt,
      IX, p. 58; cf. *Hamlet*, II. ii. 251-2)

The Return from Parnassus

Why, the wide *world*, that blesseth some with weal,
Is to our chained thoughts a darksome jail.
            (*Ibid.*, IX, p. 175; cf. *Hamlet*, II. ii. 245-6)

1603

Thomas Heywood

A Woman Kild With Kindnes

                        I will tell you Master
That which will make your heart leape from your
      brest;
Your hair to startle from your head, your eares to
      tingle.
            (II, p. 119; cf. *Hamlet*, I. v. 15-20)

New married, and new widdow'd; oh she 's dead,
And a cold *grave* must be her *Nuptiall* bed.
            (II, p. 156; cf. *Hamlet*, V. i. 254-5)

Thomas Middleton

The Phoenix

Look to 't; if *you marry*, your stubbornness is *your
      dowry.*
            (II. iii. 71-2; cf. *Hamlet*, III. i. 136-7)

ANONYMOUS

Lingua

ANAMNESTES. [*Introducing* Tragedus *and* Comedus.] Both
vice detect and *virtue beautify*,
By being death's *mirror*, and life's looking-glass.
(Dodsley's *Old English Plays* ed. by W. C. Hazlitt,
IX, p. 417; cf. *Hamlet*, III. ii. 21-6)

The Merry Divil of Edmonton

O, what a trembling horror strikes my heart!
My stiffen'd hair stands upright on my head,
As do the bristles of a porcupine.
(*Ibid.*, X, p. 209; cf. *Hamlet*, I. v. 18-20)

1604

BEAUMONT AND FLETCHER

The Woman's Prize, or the Tamer Tam'd

ROWLAND. *Come swear;* I know I am a man, and find
I may deceive my self: swear faithfully,
Swear me directly, am I Rowland?
TRANIO. Yes.
ROWLAND. Am I awake?
TRANIO. Ye are.
ROWLAND. Am I in health?
TRANIO. As far as I conceive . . .
ROWLAND. *Swear to all these.*
TRANIO. I will . . .
ROWLAND. *Let's remove our places.*
Swear it again.
(VIII, pp. 86-7; cf. *Hamlet*, I. v. 145 ff.)

GEORGE CHAPMAN

Monsieur d'Olive

D'OLIVE.   I could have wish'd
    Your Highness' presence in a private conventicle
    At what time the high point of state was handled.
DUKE. What was the point?
D'OLIVE. It was my hap to make a number there
    Myself (as every other gentleman)
    Being interested in that grave affair,
    Where I deliver'd my opinion: how well—
DUKE. *What was the matter, pray?*
D'OLIVE.   The matter, sir,
    Was of an ancient subject, and yet newly
    Call'd into question; and *'twas this in brief*:
    We sate, as I remember, all in rout,
    All sorts of men together:
    A squire and a carpenter, a lawyer and a sawyer,
    A merchant and a broker, a justice and a peasant,
    And so forth, without all difference.
DUKE. *But what was the matter?*
               (II. ii. 143-59; cf. *Hamlet*, II. ii. 86 ff.)

    They 'll say I carry a whole *forest of feathers* with me.
              (III. ii. 172; cf. *Hamlet*, III. ii. 281)

The Revenge of Bussy d'Ambois

GHOST. *Away, then! Use the means thou hast to right*
    The wrong I suffer'd . . .
GUISE. Why stand'st thou still thus, and *apply'st thine ears*
    And eyes to nothing?
CLERMONT.   *Saw you nothing there?*
GUISE. *Thou dream'st awake now; what was here to see?*

CLERMONT. *My brother's spirit, urging his revenge.*[1]
> (V. i. 96 ff.; cf. *Hamlet*, III. iv. 109 ff., also
> I. ii. 254)

> How divine *a frame*
The whole world is.
> (III. iv. 66-7; cf. *Hamlet*, II. ii. 305)

THOMAS DEKKER

The Honest Whore

I was on *meditations* spotlesse *wings*.
> (II, p. 58; cf. *Hamlet*, I. v. 29-30)

Our sins by custome, seeme (at last) but small.
> (II, p. 35; cf. *Hamlet*, III. iv. 161)

HIPOLITO. Where is *the body*?
MATHEO. *The body . . . is gone to be worm'd . . .*
> Sure her winding sheete
Was laid out fore her body, and *the wormes*
That now must feast with her, were even bespoke,
And solemnly invited like strange guests.
> (II, pp. 5-6; cf. *Hamlet*, III. vii. 12 ff.)

Perhaps this shrewd pate was mine enemies:
Las! say it were: I need not feare him now:
For all his braves, his *contumelious* breath,
His frownes (tho dagger-pointed) all his plot,
(Tho ne're so mischievous) his Italian pilles,
His quarrels, and (that common sence) his law,
See, see, they 're all eaten out; here 's not left one:
How cleane they 're pickt away! to the bare bone!
> (II, p. 56; cf. *Hamlet*, V. i. 78 ff., also
> III. i. 71-4)

[1] See p. 29.

The Honest Whore, Part II

BELLAFRONT. Seeke out thy master, th' art a fit *instrument* for him.

ORLANDO. Zownes, I hope he will not *play upon me.*
(II, p. 119; cf. *Hamlet*, III. ii. 380-1)

Westward Hoe

Let these husbands play *mad Hamlet, and cry revenge.*[1]
(II, p. 353; cf. *Hamlet*, I. v. 31)

You shall heare the poore *mouse-trapt-guilty-gentlemen* call for mercy.
(II, p. 355; cf. *Hamlet*, III. ii. 241)

John Marston

The Dutch Courtesan

Wha, ha, *ho! come, bird, come.*
(I. ii. 238; cf. *Hamlet*, I. v. 116)

Illo, ho, ho: zounds, *shall I run mad*—lose my wits!
(IV. v. 66-7; cf. *Hamlet*, I. v. 116)

The Fawn

Your father shall not say I pandarised,
Or *fondly wink'd at your affection;*
No, we 'll be wise.
(III. i. 442-4; cf. *Hamlet*, II. ii. 134-9)

GARBETZA. But what strange things does thy almanack speak of, good fool?

[1] See pp. 37-8.

HEROD. Faith, lady, very strange things! It says that some
ladies of your hair shall have feeble hams, short memories, and very weak eyesight, so that they shall mistake their own page, or even brother-in-law, sometimes
for their husbands.

      (V. i. 71 ff.; cf. *Hamlet*, II. ii. 192 ff.)

The Malcontent

Believe him not; traps to catch pole-cats.[1]

      (V. iii. 147-8; cf. *Hamlet*, I. iii. 115, 127)

Illo, ho, ho, ho! art there, old truepenny?

      (III. i. 250; cf. *Hamlet*, I. v. 116, 150)

AURELIA. *Look where the* base *wretch comes.*
[*Enter* Mendoza, *reading a sonnet.*[2]

      (I. ii. 66-7; cf. *Hamlet*, II. ii. 168)

World! 'tis the only region of death, the greatest shop
of the devil; the cruelest *prison of men.*

      (IV. ii. 25-6; cf. *Hamlet*, II. ii. 246)

Sweet women! most sweet ladies! nay, angels! . . .
O paradise! how majestical is your austerer presence!
how imperiously chaste is your more modest face! . . .
in body how delicate, in soul how witty, in discourse
how pregnant, in life how wary, in favours how judicious, in day how sociable, and in night how—O
pleasure unutterable![3]

      (I. i. 339 ff.; cf. *Hamlet*, II. ii. 310-5)

[1] See p. 118.
[2] See pp. 117-18.
[3] See p. 117.

Elder of Israel, thou honest defect of wicked nature
and obstinate ignorance, when did thy wife let thee lie
with her?[1]

> (III. i. 172-4; cf. *Hamlet*, II. ii. 413-4)

Twelve moons have suffer'd change since I beheld
The lovèd presence of my dearest lord.

> (V. iii. 56-7; cf. *Hamlet*, III. ii. 161-2)

CONDELL. I beseech you, sir, *be covered.*
SLY. *No, in good faith, for mine ease.*

> (Induction, ll. 37-8; cf. *Hamlet*, V. ii. 106)

1605

GEORGE CHAPMAN

The Widow's Tears

But let me wonder at this *frailty* yet;
Would she in so short time wear out his memory,
So soon wipe from her eyes, nay, from her heart,
Whom I myself, and this whole isle besides,
Still remember with grief.[2]

> (III. i. 112-6; cf. *Hamlet*, I. ii. 146-52)

Her officious ostentation of sorrow condemns her sincerity. When did ever woman mourn so unmeasurably,
but she did dissemble? . . . My sister may *turn Niobe*
for love; but till Niobe be turned to a marble, I'll not
despair but she may prove *a woman.*[3]

> (IV. i. 110 ff.; cf. *Hamlet*, I. ii. 146-9)

[1] See p. 118.
[2] See p. 86.
[3] See p. 87.

LYSANDER. Th'ast wept these four whole days.

ERO. Nay, by 'rlady, almost five!

LYSANDER. Look you there; near upon five whole days![1]

(V. i. 110-2; cf. *Hamlet*, III. ii. 127-32)

GEORGE CHAPMAN, BEN JONSON, JOHN MARSTON

Eastward Hoe

*The superfluity and cold meat left at their nuptials
will with bounty furnish ours.*[2]

(II. i. 164-6; cf. *Hamlet*, I. ii. 180-1)

Your father, and some one more, stole to church with
'hem in all the haste, that the *cold meat left at your
wedding might serve to furnish their nuptial table.*[3]

(III. ii. 60-3; cf. *Hamlet*, I. ii. 180-1)

HAMLET. What, coachman—my lady's coach! for shame! her
ladyship's ready to come down!

POTKIN. 'Sfoot! *Hamlet, are you mad?* . . .

GERTRUDE. *My coach,* for the love of heaven, *my coach!*
In good truth I shall swoon else . . .
[*Sings.*] *His head as white as milk, all flaxen was his
hair;
But now he is dead, and laid in his bed,
And never will come again,
God be at your labour!*[4]

(III. ii. 4 ff.; cf. *Hamlet*, IV. i. 72, 190-8,
also II. ii. 92)

[1] See p. 87.
[2] See p. 120.
[3] See p. 120.
[4] See p. 119.

Ay me! see another remnant of this unfortunate shipwreck, or some other. A woman, i' faith, a woman;
though it be almost at St. Katherine's, I discern it to
be a woman, for all her body is above the water, and
*her clothes swim about her most handsomely. O, they
bear her up most bravely!* has not a woman reason to
love the taking up of her clothes the better while she
lives, for this? Alas! how busy the rude Thames is about
her! a pox o' that wave! it will drown her, i' faith,
'twill drown her! Cry God mercy, she has 'scaped it—
I thank heaven she has 'scaped it! O how she swims
like a mermaid![1]

> (IV. i. 60-71; cf. *Hamlet*, IV. iii. 174-5)

Thomas Dekker

Northward Hoe

FEATHERSTONE. Upon your promise of secrecie.
BELLAMONT. You shall close it up like treasure of your owne,
and *your selfe shall keepe the key of it.*

> (III, p. 5; cf. *Hamlet*, I. iii. 84-6)

1606

Beaumont and Fletcher

The Woman-Hater

It comes again; New apparitions,
And tempting spirits: *Stand and reveal thy self,
Tell why thou followest me!*

> (X, p. 96; cf. *Hamlet*, I. i. 126-41, 2)

That pleasing peece of *frailtie, that we call woman.*

> (X, p. 100; cf. *Hamlet*, I. ii. 146)

[1] See p. 121.

But if you hope to try *her* truly, and satisfy yourself
what frailty is, give *her* the Test.

> (X, p. 132; cf. *Hamlet*, I. ii. 146)

COUNT. Lazarello, bestirr thy self nimbly and sodainly, and
hear me with patience [to hear].
LAZARELLO. Let me not fall from my self; *Speak I 'm bound.*
COUNT. *So art thou to revenge, when thou shalt hear.*[1]

> (X, pp. 92-3; cf. *Hamlet*, I. v. 5-8)

Full eight and twenty several Almanacks
Have been compiled, all for several years
Since first I drew this breath, four prentiships
Have I most truely served in this world:
And eight and twenty times hath Phoebus car
Run out his yearly course since.[2]

> (X, p. 90; cf. *Hamlet*, III. ii. 159-62)

John Day

The Isle of Gulls

Hath he no fellow acters in his most lamentable *com-*
micall, historicall, tragicall, musicall, *pastoriall?*

> (I, p. 86; cf. *Hamlet*, II. ii. 406-9)

John Marston

The Tragedy of Sophonisba

Chance hath so often struck
I scarce can feel. I should now *curse* the gods,
Call on the furies, stamp the patient earth.

[1] See p. 121.
[2] See p. 122.

Cleave my stretch'd cheeks *with sound*, speak from all
    sense,
But loud and full of *player's eloquence.*
                    (IV. i. 22-6; cf. *Hamlet*, II. ii. 565 ff.)

His virtue mazed me, faintness seized me all:
Some god's in kings, that will not let them fall.
                    (II. iii. 18-9; cf. *Hamlet*, IV. i. 122-4)

Thomas Middleton

A Mad World, My Masters

Clay! dost call thy captain *clay?* Indeed, *clay was made
to stop holes;* he says true.
                    (III. iii. 123-4; cf. *Hamlet*, V. i. 222-3)

Cyril Tourneur

The Atheist's Tragedy

SOLDIER. [*To* Montferrers' *Ghost.*] *Stand! Stand, I say!* No?
    Why then have at thee,
    Sir. *If you will not stand,* I'll make you fall. [*Fires.*
    Nor stand nor fall? Nay then, the devil's dam
    Has broke her husband's head, for sure *it is
    A spirit.
    It shot it through, and yet it will not fall.*[1]
                    (II. vi. p. 287; cf. *Hamlet*, I. i. 139-46)

To lose a father and, as you may think,
Be disinherited, it must be granted
*Are motives to impatience. But for death,
Who can avoid it?* And for his estate,

[1] See p. 31.

In the uncertainty of both your lives
'Twas done discreetly to confer 't upon
A known successor being the next in blood.
And one, dear nephew, whom in time to come
You shall have cause to thank. *I will not be*
Your dispossessor but your guardian.
I will supply your father's vacant place
To guide your green improvidence of youth,
And make you ripe for your inheritance.[1]

        (III. iv. p. 300; cf. *Hamlet*, I. ii. 87 ff.)

These circumstances, uncle, tell me you
Are the suspected author of those wrongs,
Whereof the lightest is more heavy than
The strongest patience can endure to bear.[2]

        (III. i. p. 293; cf. *Hamlet*, I. v. 40-1, 189-90)

          Why, was I born a coward?
He lies that says so. Yet the countenance of
A bloodless worm might ha' the courage now
To turn my blood to water.
The trembling motion of an aspen leaf
Would make me, like the shadow of that leaf,
Lie shaking under 't. *I could now commit*
A murder were it but to drink the fresh
Warm blood of him I murdered to supply
The want and weakness o' mine own,
'Tis grown so cold and phlegmatic.[3]

          (IV. iii. p. 315; cf. *Hamlet*, II. ii. 586-94, also
          III. ii. 400-2)

CHARLEMONT. [*In a churchyard.*] This grave—Perhaps the
    inhabitant was in his lifetime the possessor of his own

[1] See pp. 33-4.
[2] See p. 32.
[3] See p. 35.

desires. Yet in the midst of all his greatness and his wealth he was less rich and less contented than in this poor piece of earth lower and lesser than a cottage. For here he neither wants nor cares. Now that his body savours of corruption

He enjoys a sweeter rest than e'er he did
Amongst the sweetest pleasures of this life,
For here there's nothing troubles him.—And there
—In that grave lies another. He, perhaps,
Was in his life as full of misery
As this of happiness. And here's an end
Of both. Now both their states are equal. O
That man with so much labour should aspire
To worldly height, when in the humble earth
The world's condition's at the best, or scorn
Inferior men, since to be lower than
A worm is to be higher than a king.[1]

(IV. iii. pp. 307-8; cf. *Hamlet*, V. i. 101 ff.)

Set down the body. Pay Earth what she lent.
But she shall bear *a living monument.*

(III. i. p. 288; cf. *Hamlet*, V. i. 306)

And I am of a confident belief
That even the time, place, manner of our deaths,
Do follow Fate with that necessity
That makes us sure to die.

(I. ii. p. 251; cf. *Hamlet*, V. ii. 224-6)

Anonymous

Wily Beguild

I'll make him fly *swifter than meditation.*
(Dodsley's *Old English Plays* ed. by W. C. Hazlitt, IX, p. 222; cf. *Hamlet*, I. v. 29-30)

[1] See p. 33.

Thrice three times Sol hath slept in Thetis' lap,
Since these mine eyes beheld sweet Lelia's face.
(Ibid., IX, p. 282; cf. Hamlet, III. ii. 159-60)

1607

THOMAS HEYWOOD

Fortune by Land and Sea

Indeed *I flatter not, none flatter those*
They do not mean to gain by, 'tis the guise
Of siccophants, such great men to adore
By whom they mean to rise, *disdain the poor.*
(VI, p. 402; cf. Hamlet, III. ii. 57-63)

PHILIP MASSINGER, THOMAS MIDDLETON,
WILLIAM ROWLEY

The Old Law

There will be charges saved too; the same rosemary that
serves for the funeral will serve for the wedding.
(IV. i. 35-7; cf. Hamlet, I. ii. 180-1)

Alas, poor ghost!
(II. ii. 74; cf. Hamlet, I. v. 4)

Clerks are the most *indifferent honest* men.
(III. i. 54-5; cf. Hamlet, III. i. 122-3)

WILLIAM ROWLEY

The Birth of Merlin

Oft have I chid the winds for breathing on me.
(IV. i. 171; cf. Hamlet, I. ii. 140-2)

CLOWN. So ho, boy, so ho, so, so.
PRINCE UTER. [*Within.*] So ho, *boy*, so ho, *illo ho, illo ho.*

> (II. i. 45-6; cf. *Hamlet*, I. v. 115-6)

CYRIL TOURNEUR

The Revenger's Tragedy

For to be honest is not to be i' the world.

> (I. i. p. 346; cf. *Hamlet*, II. ii. 239-40)

VENDICE. *Shall we kill him now he's drunk?*
LUSURIOSO. Ay, best of all.
VENDICE. Why, then he will ne'er live to be sober.
LUSURIOSO. No matter, *let him reel to hell.*

> (V. i. p. 421; cf. *Hamlet*, III. iii. 89 ff.)

O you Heavens! take *this infectious spot out of my soul,*
I'll rinse it in seven waters of mine eyes![1]

> (IV. iv. p. 415; cf. *Hamlet*, III. iv. 89-91)

VENDICE. Thou sallow picture of my poisoned love.
　　　　　　　　[*Views the skull in his hand.*
My study's ornament, thou shell of death,
Once the bright face of my betrothèd lady,
When life and beauty naturally filled out
These ragged imperfections;
When two heaven-pointed diamonds were set
In those unsightly rings—then 'twas a face
So far beyond the artificial shine
Of any woman's bought complexion,
That the uprightest man (if such there be,
That sin but seven times a day) broke custom,
And made up eight with looking after her.[2]

> (I. i. p. 344; cf. *Hamlet*, V. i. 78 ff.)

[1] See p. 104.
[2] See p. 115.

Here's an eye,
Able to tempt a great man—to serve God:
A pretty hanging lip, that has forgot now to dissemble.
Methinks this mouth should make a swearer trem-
ble . . .
Does every proud and self-affecting dame
Camphire her face for this, and grieve her Maker
In sinful baths of milk, when many an infant starves
For her superfluous outside—all for this?
Who now bids twenty pounds a night? prepares
Music, perfumes, and sweetmeats? All are hush'd.
Thou may'st lie chaste now![1]

(III. iv. pp. 391-2; cf. *Hamlet*, V. i. 196-204)

1607-8

Louis Machin

The Dumb Knight

And you shall take them, *as they clip each other,*
Even in their height of sin, then damn them both,
And let them sink before they ask God pardon,
That your revenge may stretch unto their souls.
(Dodsley's *Old English Plays* ed. by W. C. Hazlitt,
X, pp. 173-4; cf. *Hamlet*, III. iii. 90 ff.)

1608

Robert Armin

The History of Two Maids of More-clack

Ile fit ye sir, *tis here*, I am tutch right, *hic & ubique*,
everywhere.

(p. 123; cf. *Hamlet*, I. i. 141, also I. v. 156)

[1] See p. 115.

The bird that greets the dawning of the daie,
Signes with his wings, the midnights parture,
And the sleetie *deaw moistning the cheekes*
Of morrowes welcome, gives earnest of the morne.
(p. 99; cf. Hamlet, I. i. 150 ff.)

My mother is an alien,
From my blood, so to *fall off*, and perish
Even in her pride of blisse.
(p. 101; cf. Hamlet, I. v. 47)

HUMIL. [*Convinced of his error in doubting his mother's
virtue.*] I appeal to sterne rigor, O you sonnes
Whose true obedience shines in majesty
While mine *more ugly then is vulcans tithye,*
Smels ranker then despised Hemlocke.
(p. 103; cf. Hamlet, III. ii. 84-5)

Was I bewitcht
That thus at hud-man blind I dallied
With her I honor'd?
(p. 104; cf. Hamlet, III. iv. 76-7)

BEAUMONT AND FLETCHER

Four Plays or Moral Representations in One

She is gone then,
Or any else, that *promises, or power,*
Gifts, or his *guilful vows* can work upon.[1]
(X, p. 338; cf. Hamlet, I. v. 41-6)

Just *such a flattery,*
With that same cunning face, that smile upon 't,

[1] See p. 54.

Oh mark it Marie, mark it seriously,
That Master smile caught me.[1]
>   (X, p. 339; cf. *Hamlet*, I. v. 106-8)

That *noble piece* ye made, and call'd it *man*.
>   (X, p. 339; cf. *Hamlet*, II. ii. 310-1)

LAVAL. Gentille, come hither: who 's that Gentlewoman?
GENTILLE. A child of mine, Sir, who observing custome,
   Is going *to the Monastery to her Prayers* . . .
LAVAL. Go on, *fair Beauty*, and *in your Orizons*
   Remember me: will ye, *fair sweet?*
>   (X, pp. 340-1; cf. *Hamlet*, III. i. 89-90)

Oh! my afflicted soul: *I cannot pray;*
And the least child that has but goodness in him
May strike my head off; so stupid are my powers:
I 'll lift mine eyes up though.[2]
>   (X, p. 353; cf. *Hamlet*, III. iii. 38 ff.)

Take him dead drunk now without repentance,
His leachery inseam'd upon him.[3]
>   (X, p. 351; cf. *Hamlet*, III. iii. 88 ff., also
>   III. iv. 91-2)

By this we plainly view the two *imposthumes*
That choke a kingdoms welfare; *Ease*, and Wantonness.
>   (X, p. 355; cf. *Hamlet*, III. viii. 27)

Wit at Several Weapons

>   *If I durst speak,*
Or could be believ'd when I speak,

[1] See p. 55.
[2] See p. 56.
[3] See p. 55.

*What a tale could I tell, to make hair stand upright
now!*
(IX, p. 107; cf. Hamlet, I. v. 13-20)

John Webster

Appius and Virginia

This sight hath stiffned all *my operant powers*.
(V. ii. 108; cf. Hamlet, III. ii. 178)

1609

George Chapman

May-Day

Come, be not *retrograde to our desires*.
(III. iii. 196; cf. Hamlet, I. ii. 114)

Nathaniel Field

A Woman is a Weathercock

O my divining spirit.
(Dodsley's *Old English Plays* ed. by W. C. Hazlitt,
XI, p. 82; cf. *Hamlet*, I. v. 40)

For I tell thee, reader, if thou be'st ignorant, *a play*
is not so idle a thing as thou art, but *a mirror of men's
lives and actions*.
(Ibid., XI, p. 8; cf. Hamlet, III. ii. 21-6)

Ben Jonson

The Case is Altered

Deare Angelo, you are not every man,
But *one, whome my election hath design'd*,

As the true proper object of my soule:
I urge not this t' insinuate my desert,
Or supple your tri'd temper, with soft phrases;
True friendship lothes such oyly complement:
But from th' aboundance of that love, that flowes
Through all my spirits, is my speech enforc'd.

> (I. vi. 30-7; cf. *Hamlet*, III. ii. 55 ff.)

1610

BEAUMONT AND FLETCHER

Monsieur Thomas

The only temper'd spirit, *Scholar, Souldier,*
Courtier; and all in one piece!

> (IV, p. 115; cf. *Hamlet*, III. i. 156)

Philaster

Yes, with *my Fathers spirit*: It's here O King!
A dangerous spirit; now he tells me King,
I was a Kings heir, bids me be a King,
And whispers to me, these be all my Subjects.
'Tis strange, he will not let me sleep, but dives
Into my fancy, and there gives me shapes
That kneel, and do me service, cry me King:
But *I'le suppress him, he's a factious spirit,*
And will undo me.[1]

> (I, p. 82; cf. *Hamlet*, II. ii. 615-20, also III. ii. 94-6)

                    Have I stood
Naked, alone the shock of many fortunes?

---

[1] See pp. 58-9.

Have I seen *mischiefs numberless, and mighty*
Grow like a sea upon me?

> (I, p. 114; cf. *Hamlet*, III. i. 59)

PHILASTER. Oh, but thou dost not know what 'tis *to die.*
BELLARIO.   Yes, I do know my Lord;
　'Tis less than to be born; *a lasting sleep,*
　A quiet resting from all jealousie;
　A thing we all pursue . . .
PHILASTER. But *there are pains,* false boy,
　For perjur'd souls.

> (I, pp. 110-1; cf. *Hamlet*, III. i. 64-5)

Mark but the King *how pale he looks with fear.*
Oh! this same whorson Conscience, *how it jades us!*

> (I, p. 80; cf. *Hamlet*, III. ii. 245-7)

　　　　　　　　But how can I,
Look to be heard of gods, that must be just,
Praying upon the ground I hold by wrong?[1]

> (I, p. 99; cf. *Hamlet*, III. iii. 51-5)

　　　　　　　This earth you tread upon
(A dowry as you hope with this fair Princess,
Whose memory I bow to) was not left
By my dead Father (Oh, I had a Father)
To your inheritance, and I up and living,
Having my self about me and my sword,
The souls of all my name, and memories,
These arms and some few friends, besides the gods,
To part so calmly with it, and sit still,
And say I might have been![2]

> (I, p. 80; cf. *Hamlet*, III. viii. 43-6)

[1] See p. 63.
[2] See p. 57.

The Tragedy of Valentinian

Break not the *goodly frame* ye build in anger.
(IV, p. 80; cf. Hamlet, II. ii. 305)

JOHN MARSTON

The Insatiate Countess

Believe it is a wrong unto the gods.
They sail against the wind that wail the dead.[1]
(I. i. 39-40; cf. Hamlet, I. ii. 101-3)

She had a lord,

Jealous the air should ravish her chaste looks.[2]
(V. i. 169-70; cf. Hamlet, I. ii. 140-2)

With tears, *like Niobe.*
(V. ii. 70; cf. Hamlet, I. ii. 149)

When I was absent then *her gallèd eyes*
Would have shed April showers.[3]
(II. iv. 33-4; cf. Hamlet, I. ii. 154-6)

My lord of Cyprus, *do not mock my grief.*[4]
(I. i. 34; cf. Hamlet, I. ii. 177)

As *swift as thought* fly I to wish thee aid.
(III. ii. 71; cf. Hamlet, I. v. 29-30)

A *player's passion* I'll believe hereafter,

[1] See p. 82.
[2] See p. 84.
[3] See p. 83.
[4] See p. 81.

And in a tragic scene weep for *old Priam*,
When *fell-revenging Pyrrhus* with supposed
And artificial wounds mangles his breast.[1]

> (I. i. 122-4; cf. *Hamlet*, II. ii. 483-6, 565-8)

His heart hath wrestled with death's pangs,
From whose stern cave none tracts a backward path.[2]

> (I. i. 41-2; cf. *Hamlet*, III. i. 79-80)

The tapers that stood on her husband's hearse
    Isabel advances to a second bed.
Is it not wondrous strange for to rehearse
    She should so soon forget her husband, *dead*
One hour? for if the husband's life once fade,
Both love and husband in one grave are laid.[3]

> (I. i. 132-7; cf. *Hamlet*, III. ii. 128-30, 218-9)

Did'st thou not *kill him drunk?* . . .
Thou should'st, or *in the embraces of his lust.*

> (V. i. 86-7; cf. *Hamlet*, III. iii. 89-90)

A donative he hath of every god:
Apollo gave him locks; *Jove his high front;*
The god of eloquence his flowing speech;
The feminine deities strew'd all their bounties
And beauty on his face; that eye was Juno's;
Those lips were hers that won the golden ball;
That virgin-blush, Diana's.

> (I. i. 62-8; cf. *Hamlet*, III. iv. 55-62)

I am not mad—I can hear, I can see, I can feel!

> (I. i. 363; cf. *Hamlet*, III. iv. 139-44)

[1] See p. 82.
[2] See p. 82.
[3] See p. 83.

A host of angels be thy convey hence.
>   (V. i. 226; cf. *Hamlet*, V. ii. 365)

THOMAS MIDDLETON

The Roaring Girl

>   Albeit mine eyes
> Are blest by thine, yet this so strange disguise
> *Holds me with fear and wonder.*
>   (I. i. 66-8; cf. *Hamlet*, I. i. 44)

Since last I saw him, *twelve months three times told*
The moon hath drawn through her light silver bow.
>   (III. ii. 125-6; cf. *Hamlet*, III. ii. 161-2)

He that can take me for a male musician,
I can't choose but make him my *instrument*,
And play upon him.
>   (IV. i. 217-9; cf. *Hamlet*, III. ii. 380-1)

1611

BEAUMONT AND FLETCHER

The Maids Tragedy

Or *like* another *Niobe* I 'le weep till I am water.
>   (I, p. 51; cf. *Hamlet*, I. ii. 149)

I have observ'd, *your words fall from your tongue*
Wildly; and all your carriage,
Like one that strove to shew his merry mood,
When he were ill dispos'd.[1]

>   (I, p. 36; cf. *Hamlet*, I. v. 133)

[1] See p. 64.

KING. Well, *I will try him*, and if this be true
    I 'le pawn my life I 'le find it; if 't be false,
    And that you clothe your hate in such a lie,
    You shall hereafter *doat in your own house*, not in
        the Court.
CALIANAX. Why if it be a lie,
    Mine ears are false; for I 'le be sworn I heard it:
    Old men are good for nothing; you were best
    Put me to death for hearing, and free him
    For meaning of it; *you would ha' trusted me*
    Once, but the time is altered.[1]

                      (I, p. 52; cf. *Hamlet*, II. ii. 153-67, also
                      III. i. 133-4)

                              I must kill him,
And I will do 't bravely: the meer joy
Tells me I merit in it: *yet I must not*
Thus tamely do it as he sleeps: that were
To rock him to another world: my vengeance
Shall take him waking, and then lay before him
The number of his wrongs and punishments.
I 'le shake his sins like furies, till I waken
His evil Angel, his sick Conscience:
And then I 'le strike him dead.
                    (I, p. 61; cf. *Hamlet*, III. iii. 74 ff.)

Out with thy sword; and hand in hand with me
Rush to the Chamber of this hated King,
And *sink him with the weight of all his sins to hell*
    for ever.
                    (I, p. 59; cf. *Hamlet*, III. iii. 88-95)

                  Stir not, if thou dost,
I 'le take thee unprepar'd; thy fears upon thee,
    That make thy sins look double, *and so send thee*

---

[1] See p. 66.

(By my revenge, I will) *to look those torments*
Prepar'd for such black souls.
> (I, p. 62; cf. *Hamlet*, III. iii. 91-5)

If thy hot soul had substance with thy blood,
I would kill that too.
> (I, p. 63; cf. *Hamlet*, III. iii. 94-5)

MELANTIUS. I would speak loud; here's one should *thunder*
    to 'em . . .
Thou hast death about thee: h'as undone thine honour,
poyson'd thy vertue, and *of a lovely rose, left thee*
a canker . . .
        Speak you whore, speak truth,
Or by the dear soul of thy sleeping Father,
This sword shall be thy lover: tell, or I 'le kill thee:
And when thou hast told all, thou wilt deserve it.
EVADNE. *You will not murder me! . . . Help!*[1]
> (I, p. 46; cf. *Hamlet*, III. iv. 21-2, 40 ff.)

        For as you are meer man,
I dare as easily kill you for this deed,
As you dare think to do it; but *there is*
Divinity about you, that strikes dead
My rising passions, as you are my King,
I fall before you.
> (I, p. 33; cf. *Hamlet*, IV. i. 122-4)

NATHANIEL FIELD

Amends For Ladies

One-and-thirty good morrows to the fairest, wisest,
richest widow *that ever conversation coped withal.*
> (Dodsley's *Old English Plays* ed. by W. C. Hazlitt,
> XI, p. 99; cf. *Hamlet*, III. ii. 56)

[1] See pp. 69-70.

Thomas Middleton

A Chaste Maid in Cheapside

O, how my offences wrestle with my repentance!
It hath scarce breath;
Still my adulterous guilt hovers aloft,
And with her black wings beats down all my prayers
Ere they be half-way up.

> (V. i. 73-7; cf. *Hamlet*, III. iii. 36-40)

John Webster

The White Devil

> I 'le close mine eyes,
> And in a melancholicke thought I 'le frame
> Her figure 'fore me . . . [*Enter* Isabella's *Ghost.*
> *Thought, as a subtile Jugler, makes us deeme*
> *Things, supernaturall, which have cause*
> *Common as sickenesse. 'Tis my melancholy.*

> (IV. i. 104 ff.; cf. *Hamlet*, II. ii. 618-20)

T' have poison'd his praier booke, or a paire of beades,
The pummell of his saddle, his looking-glasse,
Or th' handle of his racket—ô that, that!
That while he had bin bandying at Tennis,
He might have sworne himselfe to hell, and strooke
His soule into the hazzard!

> (V. i. 67-72; cf. *Hamlet*, III. iii. 91-5)

There 's Rosemarie for you, and Rue for you,
Hearts-ease for you. I pray make much of it,
I have left more for my selfe.[1]

> (V. iv. 70-3; cf. *Hamlet*, IV. i. 173 ff.)

[1] See pp. 91-92.

1612

Beaumont and Fletcher

Cupid's Revenge

Leave her to Heaven, brave Cosin, they shall tell her
how she has sinn'd against 'em, my hand shall never be
stain'd with such base bloud: live *wicked Mother*: that
reverend Title be your pardon, for I will use no extremity against you, but *leave you to Heaven*.

(IX, p. 287; cf. *Hamlet*, I. v. 86)

Thomas Dekker

Match Me in London

Yet I have cause to rave, *my wits like Bels*
Are backward rung.

(IV, p. 209; cf. *Hamlet*, III. i. 162-3)

Sweare thou art not mine,
That when I see thy heart drunke with hot oathes,
This Feind may pitch thee reeling into Hell,
Sweare that thou art not mine.

(IV, pp. 209-10; cf. *Hamlet*, III. iii. 91-5)

On Kings shoulders stand
The heads of the Colossie of the Goddes
(*Above the reach of Traitors*) were the beds
Of twenty thousand Snakes layd in this bosome,
There's thunder in our lookes to breake them all.

(IV, p. 202; cf. *Hamlet*, IV. i. 121-4)

Thomas Heywood

The Silver Age

Bee'st thou infernall hagge, or fiend incarnate,
I conjure thee.

(III, p. 119; cf. *Hamlet*, I. iv. 40)

1613

Beaumont and Fletcher

The Honest Man's Fortune

DUBOIS. Let his Lordship give me but his honorable word
for my life, I 'll kill him as he walks.
LAVERDUE. Or pistoll him as he sits at meat.
LAPOOP. *Or at game.*
LAVERDUE. *Or as he is drinking.*

(X, p. 229; cf. *Hamlet*, III. iii. 89-91)

The Scornful Lady

Have patience Sir until our fellow Nicholas be de-
ceast, that is, *asleep:* for so the word is taken: *to sleep
to dye, to dye to sleep, a very figure* Sir.

(I, p. 245; cf. *Hamlet*, III. i. 60 ff., also II. ii. 97-8)

I will run mad first, and if that get not pitty,
I 'le drown my self to a most dismal ditty.

(I, p. 272; cf. *Hamlet*, IV. iii. 176-82)

The Two Noble Kinsmen

EMILIA. [*Comparing the pictures of* Palamon *and* Arcite.]
What an eye!
Of what a fiery sparkle, and quick sweetness:

Has this young Prince! here Love himself sits smiling,
Just such another wanton Ganimead,
Set Love a fire with, and enforc'd the god
Snatch up the goodly Boy, and set him by him
A shining constellation: *what a brow*,
Of what a spacious Majesty he carries!
Arch'd like the great ey'd Juno's, but far sweeter,
Smoother than Pelops Shoulder . . .
Palamon
Is but his foil, to him, a mere dull shadow,
He 's swarth, and meagre, of an eye as heavy
As if he had lost his mother.[1]

(IX, pp. 351-2; cf. Hamlet, III. iv. 53 ff.)

I have forgot it quite; the burden on 't was *Down
A Down a.*[2]

(IX, p. 356; cf. Hamlet, IV. i. 169-70)

Then she talk'd of you, Sir;
That you must lose your head to morrow morning
And she must gather Flowers to bury you,
And see the house made handsome, then *she sung
Nothing but willow, willow, willow*, and between
Ever was, Palamon, fair Palamon,
And Palamon, was a tall young man. *The place
Was knee deep where she sate; her careless Tresses,
A wreath of Bull-rush rounded; about her stuck
Thousand fresh Water Flowers of several colours.
That methought she appear'd like the fair Nymph
That feeds the lake with waters*, or as Iris
Newly dropt down from heaven; *Rings she made
Of Rushes that grew by*, and to 'em spoke
The prettiest posies: thus our true love 's ty'd,

[1] See p. 109.
[2] See p. 90.

This you may loose, not me, and many a one:
And then she wept, *and sung again*, and sigh'd,
And with the same breath smil'd, and kist her hand.[1]

(IX, pp. 348-9; cf. *Hamlet*, IV. iii. 165 ff.)

GEORGE CHAPMAN

The Tragedy of Chabot

PROCTOR-GENERAL. It is not unknown to you, my very good
lords the Judges, and indeed to all the world, *for I
will make short work*, since your honourable ears need
not be enlarged—*I speak by a figure*—with prolix
enumeration, how infinitely the King hath favoured
this ill-favoured traitor . . .

CHANCELLOR. You express your oratory, Master Proctor;
I pray *come presently to the matter*.

(III. ii. 1 ff.; cf. *Hamlet*, II. ii. 90 ff.)

Brutus, the loved son, hath stabbed *Caesar* with a
bodkin. Oh, *what brute may be compared to him*, and
in what particulars may this crime be exemplified?

(III. ii. 58-61; cf. *Hamlet*, III. ii. 105-7)

THOMAS HEYWOOD

The Brazen Age

All men must dye, thou, he, and every one,
Yea I my selfe must: but *I'le tell you that
Shall stiffe your haire, your eyes start from your heads,*
Print fixt amazement in your wondring fronts,
Yea and astonish all.

(III, p. 202; cf. *Hamlet*, I. ii. 72, also I. v. 15-20)

[1] See pp. 89-90.

The Second Part of the Iron Age

[*Enter* Aeneas *followed by* Hectors *ghost.*
AENEAS. *What art thou that with such a grim aspect,*
In this black night so darke and turbulent,
Haunts me in every corner of my house.

> (III, p. 383; cf. *Hamlet*, I. i. 46-9)

SINON. [*Signalling from the walls of Troy.*] *The black*
    darknesse falne,
And rould o're all the world, as well the Poles,
As the great Ocean, and the earth: now 's the time
For tragicke slaughter, *clad in gules and sables,*
To spring out of Hels jawes, and play strang reaks
In sleepy Troy.

> (III, p. 379; cf. *Hamlet*, II. ii. 465 ff.)

My brayne about againe, for thou hast found
New project now to worke on.

> (III, p. 408; cf. *Hamlet*, II. ii. 605)

CLITEMNESTRA. *Thou a sonne?*
ORESTES. *The name I am ashamed of . . .*
        [*Enter Ghost of* Agamemnon.
  Lady see.
CLITEMNESTRA. *See what?* Thy former murder *makes thee*
    mad.
ORESTES. [*To Ghost.*] Rest Ghost in peace, I now am sat-
    isfied,
And neede no further witnesse. [*To his mother.*] *Saw*
    you nothing?
CLITEMNESTRA. *What should I see save this sad spectacle,*
Which blood-shootes both mine eyes.

ORESTES. *And nothing else?* . . .
    Mine eyes are clearer sighted then, and see
    Into thy bosome. Murdresse.[1]
        (III, pp. 421-3; cf. *Hamlet*, III. iv. 14-16, 105 ff.)

ROBERT TAILOR

The Hog Hath Lost His Pearl

I have attain'd what doth adorn man's being,
That precious gem of reason, by which solely
We are discern'd from rude and brutish beasts,
No other difference being 'twixt us and them.
    (Dodsley's *Old English Plays* ed. by W. C. Hazlitt,
    XI, pp. 481-2; cf. *Hamlet*, III. viii. 35-9)

1614

BEAUMONT AND FLETCHER

The Night-Walker, or the Little Thief

A sad wedding,
Her grave must be her Bridal bed!
        (VII, p. 326; cf. *Hamlet*, V. i. 254-5)

1615

R. A.

The Valiant Welshman

Like Niobe, in teares.
            (I. i. 8; cf. *Hamlet*, I. ii. 149)

[1] See pp. 104-6.

Then *my propheticke spirite* tels me true.
> (III. ii. 10; cf. *Hamlet*, I. v. 40)

And not from *that which reason or discourse*
Proudly from beasts doth challenge, as from man.
> (I. iv. 62-3; cf. *Hamlet*, III. viii. 35-9)

CLOWN. My masters, and fellow questmen, this is the point, we are to search out the course of law, *whether this man* that has hangde himselfe, *be accessary to his own death or no* . . . I put this point to you, whether every one that hangs himselfe, be willing to die or no?

SECOND NEIGHBOR. I, I, sure he is willing.

CLOWN. I say no, for the hangman hangs himselfe, and yet he is not willing to die.

THIRD NEIGHBOR. How dos the hangman hang himselfe?

CLOWN. I mary dos he, sir; for if he have not a man to doe his office for him, he must hang himselfe: *ergo*, every man that hangs himselfe is not willing to die.

FIRST NEIGHBOR. He sayes very true indeed: but now sir, being dead, who shall answere the King for his subject?

CLOWN. Mary sir, he that hangd his subject.

SECOND NEIGHBOR. That was himselfe.

THIRD NEIGHBOR. No sir, I doe thinke *it was the halter that hangde him*.

CLOWN. I, in a sort, but *that was, se offendendo*, for it may be, he meant to have broke the halter, and *the halter held him out of his owne defence*.

FIRST NEIGHBOR. But is not the Ropemaker in danger that made it?

CLOWN. No, for hee goes backeward, when tis made, and therefore cannot see before, what will come after; neyther is the halter in fault, for hee might urge the halter, *nolens volens*, (as the learned say) neyther is he in fault, because his time was come that he should

be hanged: and therefore I doe conclude that he was
conscious and guiltlesse of his owne death: Moreover,
*he was a Lord, and a Lord in his owne precinct has
authority to hang and draw himselfe.*[1]

(IV. iii. 69-103; cf. *Hamlet*, V. i. 1-26)

1616

BEAUMONT AND FLETCHER

The Bloody Brother

Fear not, *kill him* good Captain, any way dispatch
Him, my body's honor'd with that sword that through
   me,
Sends his black soul to Hell.

(IV, p. 310; cf. *Hamlet*, III. iii. 93-5)

1617

BEAUMONT AND FLETCHER

The Queen of Corinth

I know what 'tis you point at,
The Prince Theanor's love; let not that cheat you;
*His vows were but meer Courtship; all his service
But practice how to entrap a credulous Lady:*
Or grant it serious, yet you must remember
*He's not to love, but where the Queen his Mother
Must give allowance, which to you is barr'd up:*
And therefore study to forget that ever
You cherisht such a hope.[2]

(VI, p. 6; cf. *Hamlet*, I. iii. 115-20, also I. iii. 16-24)

[1] See pp. 110-12.
[2] See p. 96.

The Tragedy of Thierry and Theodoret

Oh my presage! Father.

(X, p. 38; cf. Hamlet, I. v. 40)

Throw all the mischiefs on him that thy self,
Or woman worse than thou art, have invented,
And *kill him drunk, or doubtfull.*

(X, p. 5; cf. Hamlet, III. iii. 89)

THEODORET. Witness the daily Libels, almost Ballads . . .
Are made upon your lust . . .

Now you would blush,
But your black tainted blood dare not appear
For fear I should fright that too.

BRUNHALT. O ye gods! . . . *Art thou a son?*

THEODORET. *The more my shame is of so bad a mother,*
And more your wretchedness you let me be so;
But woman, for a mothers name hath left me
Since you have left your honor; *Mend these ruins,*
And build again that broken fame, and fairly;
Your most intemperate fires have burnt . . .

And lest Art
Should loose her self in act, *to call back custome,*
Leave these, and live *like Niobe.* I told you how
And *when your eyes have dropt away remembrance*
Of what you were. I'm your Son! performe it.[1]

(X, pp. 3-4; cf. Hamlet, III. iv. 14 ff., also I. ii. 149)

Thomas Middleton

A Fair Quarrel

She's but woman

Whose *frailty* let in death to all mankind.[2]

(II. i. 28-9; cf. Hamlet, I. ii. 146)

[1] See pp. 106-7.
[2] See p. 74.

PHYSICIAN. [*Referring to his sister.*] Look you, mistress,
    here 's your closet; put in
What you please, *you ever keep the key of it.*
            (II. ii. 65-6; cf. *Hamlet*, I. iii. 85-6)

False! do not say 't, for honour's goodness, do not!
You never could be so. He I call'd father
Deserv'd you at your best, when youth and merit
Could boast at highest in you; y' had no grace
Or virtue that he match'd not, no delight
That you invented but he sent it crown'd
To your full-wishing soul.[1]
            (II. i. 189-95; cf. *Hamlet*, I. v. 47-50)

'Tis no prison where the mind is free.
            (I. i. 399; cf. *Hamlet*, II. ii. 245-52)

            I am too full of *conscience,*
Knowledge, and patience to give justice to 't;
So careful of my eternity, which consists
Of upright actions, that *unless I knew*
It were a truth I stood for, any coward
Might make my breast his foot-pace.[2]
            (II. i. 9-14; cf. *Hamlet*, III. i. 78-83)

One master *Chough,* a Cornish gentleman;
Has as much land of his own fee-simple
As a crow can fly over in half a day.
            (I. i. 424-6; cf. *Hamlet*, V. ii. 86-9)

[1] See p. 75.
[2] See p. 73.

1617-8

Thomas Middleton

The Mayor of Queenborough

There's nothing makes man feel his miseries
But knowledge only: reason, that is plac'd
For man's director, is his chief afflictor.

> (I. i. 125-7; cf. *Hamlet*, II. ii. 251-2)

Comedians, tragedians, tragi-comedians, comi-tragedi-
ans, pastorists, humourists, clownists, satirists: we have
them, sir, from the hug to the smile, from the smile
to the laugh, from the laugh to the handkerchief.[1]

> (V. i. 75-8; cf. *Hamlet*, II. ii. 406-10)

And what a little ground shall death now teach you
To be content withal!

> (V. ii. 168-9; cf. *Hamlet*, V. i. 114-6)

1618

Beaumont and Fletcher

The Loyal Subject

> He will not come, Sir;
> *I found him at his Prayers,* there he tells me
> The Enemy shall take him, *fit for Heaven.*

> (III, p. 93; cf. *Hamlet*, III. iii. 86)

[1] See p. 98.

Anonymous

Swetnam, the Woman-Hater, Arraigned by Women

I will follow thee with *swifter speed,*
Then meditation.

(p. 58; cf. *Hamlet*, I. v. 29-30)

Therefore what shape or humor I assume,
Take you no notice that I am the Prince.

(p. 17; cf. *Hamlet*, I. v. 170 ff.)

1619

Beaumont and Fletcher

The Custom of the Country

'Tis most true,
That he's an excellent *Scholar*, and he knows it;
An exact *Courtier*, and he knows that too;
He has fought thrice, and come off still with honour.

(I, p. 318; cf. *Hamlet*, III. i. 156)

Those too many *excellencies*, that feed
Your pride, *turn to a Pleurisie*, and kill
That which should nourish vertue.

(I, p. 321; cf. *Hamlet*, IV. iii. 115-7)

The Humorous Lieutenant

This *dull root* pluckt from *Lethe* flood.

(II, p. 343; cf. *Hamlet*, I. v. 32-3)

I am reading, Sir, of a short Treatise here,
That's call'd the Vanity of Lust: has your Grace seen
it?

He says here, that an Old Mans loose desire
Is like the Glow-worms light, the Apes so wonder'd
    at . . .
And in another place he calls their loves,
Faint Smells of dying Flowers, carry no comforts;
They 're doting, stinking foggs, so thick and muddy,
Reason with all his beams cannot beat through 'em.
                    (II, pp. 350-1; cf. *Hamlet*, II. ii. 198-201)

LEONTIUS. You are cozen'd.
DEMETRIUS. And am most miserable.
LEONTIUS. *There 's no man so, but he that makes himself so.*
                    (II, p. 297; cf. *Hamlet*, II. ii. 251-2)

The Little French Lawyer

Have I a memory?
A Cause, and Will to do?
                    (III, p. 423; cf. *Hamlet*, III. viii. 45-6)

PHILIP MASSINGER

The Fatal Dowry

                    Fie, no more of this!
You have outwept a woman, noble Charalois.
No man but has or must bury a father.[1]
                    (III, p. 395; cf. *Hamlet*, I. ii. 89-94)

                    Heaven! you weep:
And I could do so too, but that I know
There 's more expected from the son and friend
Of *him whose fatal loss now shakes our natures*,
Than sighs or tears.[2]
                    (III, p. 365; cf. *Hamlet*, I. iv. 51-6, also I. ii. 89 ff.)

[1] See p. 76.
[2] See p. 76.

Oh, my heart!
Hold yet a little.[1]

(III, p. 435; cf. *Hamlet*, I. v. 93)

1620

BEAUMONT AND FLETCHER

The Double Marriage

And if 't be possible there can be added
Wings to your swift desire of just revenge,
Hear.

(VI, p. 401; cf. *Hamlet*, I. v. 29-31)

Oh my prophetique soul!

(VI, p. 353; cf. *Hamlet*, I. v. 40)

PHILIP MASSINGER

The Virgin-Martyr

That fear is base,
Of death, when that death doth but life displace
Out of her house of earth; you only dread
The stroke, and not *what follows when you 're dead;*
There 's the great fear, indeed.

(I, pp. 45-6; cf. *Hamlet*, III. i. 65-8)

1621

BEAUMONT AND FLETCHER

The Pilgrim

ALINDA.   *Is that revenge,*
To slight your cause, and *Saint your enemy,*

[1] See p. 77.

Clap the Doves wings of downy peace unto him,
And *let him soar to Heaven*, whilst you are sighing?
Is this revenge?

RODERIGO. I would have him die.

ALINDA. Prepar'd thus?
The blessing of a Father never reach'd it:
His contemplation now scorns ye, contemns ye,
And all the tortures ye can use. Let him die thus;
And these that know and love revenge will laugh at
ye . . .
This man ye rock asleep, and all your rages
Are Requiems to his parting soul, meer Anthems . . .

RODERIGO. What would'st thou have me? . . .

ALINDA. *When he appears a subject fit for anger,*
And fit for you, his pious Armour off,
His hopes no higher than your sword may reach at,
Then strike, and then ye know revenge; then take it.
(V, pp. 179-80; cf. *Hamlet*, III. iii. 84-95)

ALINDA. [*Feigning madness.*] And gaffer, here's a *Crow-*
flower, and a Dazie.
(V, p. 197; cf. *Hamlet*, IV. i. 182, also IV. iii. 168)

ALPHONSO. How comes this English mad man here?

MASTER. Alas, that's no question;
They are mad every where, Sir.
(V, p. 209; cf. *Hamlet*, V. i. 156-62)

JOHN FORD, WILLIAM ROWLEY, THOMAS DEKKER

The Witch of Edmonton

> *Get you to your nunnery;*
There freeze in your old cloister . . .
Go, go thy ways.
(III, pp. 185-6; cf. *Hamlet*, III. i. 121 ff.)

1622

BEAUMONT AND FLETCHER

The Prophetess

If Emperours flesh have this savour, what will mine do,
When I am rotten?

> (V, p. 340; cf. *Hamlet*, V. i. 209)

The Sea Voyage

Some five dayes hence that blessed hour comes
Most happy to me, that knit *this hand* to my dear hus-
bands,
And both our hearts in mutual bands.

> (IX, p. 42; cf. *Hamlet*, III. ii. 163-4)

PHILIP MASSINGER

The Maid of Honour

How willingly, like Cato,
Could I tear out my bowels, rather than
Look on the conqueror's insulting face;
But that *religion, and the horrid dream*
To be suffer'd in the other world, denies it!

> (III, p. 44; cf. *Hamlet*, III. i. 65-8)

O more than impious times! when not alone
Subordinate ministers of justice are
Corrupted and seduced, but *kings themselves,*
The greater wheels by which the lesser move,
Are broken, or disjointed!

> (III, p. 66; cf. *Hamlet*, III. iii. 17-22)

1623

BEAUMONT AND FLETCHER

The Lover's Progress

CLEANDER. [*Seeing the Ghost of the Host.*] He is not dead,
    he's here: *how pale he looks!*
                    (V, p. 115; cf. *Hamlet*, III. iv. 124)

THOMAS DEKKER

The Wonder of a Kingdom

All this world's a prison.
                    (IV, p. 235; cf. *Hamlet*, II. ii. 246)

That any held so bravely up his head,
In such a *sea of troubles* (that come rowling
One on anothers necke).
                    (IV, p. 230; cf. *Hamlet*, III. i. 59)

For when death sits even almost on her browes,
She spreads her armes abroad, to welcome him,
When in my bridall-bed I finde a grave.
                    (IV, p. 244; cf. *Hamlet*, V. i. 254-5)

PHILIP MASSINGER

The Bondman

O my prophetic soul!
                    (II, p. 77; cf. *Hamlet*, I. v. 40)

This goodly frame of concord.
                    (II, p. 78; cf. *Hamlet*, II. ii. 305)

John Webster

The Devil's Law-Case

Wit and *a woman*
Are two *very fraile* things.
                    (I. ii. 222-3; cf. *Hamlet*, I. ii. 146)

You that dwell neere these graves and vaults,
Which oft doe hide Physicians faults,
Note *what a small Roome does suffice,*
To expresse mens good—their vanities
Would fill more volume in small hand,
Than all the Evidence of Church-land.
                    (II. iii. 115-20; cf. *Hamlet*, V. i. 114-6)

1624

Beaumont and Fletcher

A Wife for a Moneth

But that thy Queen
Is of that excellent honesty,
And guarded with Divinity about her,
No loose thought can come near, nor flame unhal-
lowed,
I would so right myself.
                    (V, p. 46; cf. *Hamlet*, IV. i. 122-4)

ROBERT DAVENPORT

A City Nightcap

> *Let me send her now*
> *To th' divel, with all her sins upon her head.*
> (*Old English Plays, New Series*, ed. by A. H.
> Bullen, III, p. 110; cf. *Hamlet*, III. iii. 89-95)

THOMAS HEYWOOD

The Captives

Nowe in the name of heaven, *what art thou? Speake.*
> (IV. ii. 106; cf. *Hamlet*, I. i. 46-9)

About it brayne and in good tyme.
> (IV. ii. 47; cf. *Hamlet*, II. ii. 605)

> *Strangle him*
With all his sinnes about him. T' were not elce
A revendge woorthe my fury.
> (III. iii. 71-3; cf. *Hamlet*, III. iii. 89-95)

Sure, syr, it was som shipp of passengers,
For see you not too women? Dainty ducks!
Would they coold swime as ducks can . . .
Still theire coates beare them upp, keepe them aloft.
> (I. iii. 142 ff.; cf. *Hamlet*, IV. iii. 174-5)

PHILIP MASSINGER

The Parliament of Love

                    A hurtful vow
Is in the breach of it better commended,
Than in the keeping.
                    (II, p. 284; cf. *Hamlet*, I. iv. 15-16)

1625

PHILIP MASSINGER

A New Way to Pay Old Debts

                    Is't for your ease,
You keep your hat off?
                    (III, p. 532; cf. *Hamlet*, V. ii. 106)

1626

BEAUMONT AND FLETCHER

The Fair Maid of the Inn

CESARIO. Interpret not Clarissa, my true zeal
    In giving you counsel, to transcend the bounds
    That should confine a brother; 'tis your honor,
    And peace of mind (which honor last will leave you)
    I labor to preserve . . .
                    Excuse me,
    As you would do a Lapidary, whose whole fortunes
    Depend upon the safety of one Jewel,
    If he think no case precious enough
    To keep it in full lustre . . .

CLARISSA.   I see brother
    The mark you shoot at, and much thank your love;
    But for my Virgin Jewel which is brought
    In comparison with your Diamond, rest assur'd
    It shall not fall in such a workmans hands
    Whose ignorance or malice shall have power
    To cast one cloud upon it, but still keep
    Her native splendor . . .
CESARIO. Yet let me tell you, (but still with that love,
    I wish to increase between us) that *you are
    Observ'd* against the gravity long maintain'd
    In Italy (*where to see a maid unmasqu'd
    Is held a blemish*) *to be over-frequent
    In giving or receiving visits* . . .
                             You are fair,
    And *beauty draws temptations on* . . .
CLARISSA.   If I then borrow
    A little of the boldness of his temper,
    Imparting it to such as may deserve it;
    (*However indulgent to your selves, you brothers
    Allow no part of freedom to your Sisters*)
    I hope 'twill not pass for a crime in me,
    To grant access and speech to noble suitors;
    *And you escape for innocent, that descend
    To a thing so far beneath you.*[1]

      (IX, pp. 144-6; cf. *Hamlet*, I. iii. 29-51, 91-3)

The Noble Gentleman

        There he goes,
That was *the fairest hope the French Court bred*,
The worthiest and the sweetest temper'd spirit,
The truest, and the valiantest, the best of judgment,
Till most unhappy I: sever'd those virtues,

[1] See pp. 93-5.

And turn'd his wit wild with a coy denial,
Which heaven forgive me, and be pleas'd, O heaven
To give again his senses.

> (VIII, p. 182; cf. *Hamlet*, III. i. 155-66)

PHILIP MASSINGER

The Roman Actor

I once observed,
In a tragedy of ours, in which a murder
Was acted to the life, a guilty hearer,
Forced by the terror of a wounded conscience,
To make discovery of that which torture
Could not wring from him. Nor can it appear
Like an impossibility, but that
Your father, looking on a covetous man
Presented on the stage, as in a mirror,
May see his own deformity, and loath it.

> (II, p. 356; cf. *Hamlet*, II. ii. 605-11, also
> III. ii. 21-6)

Tremble to think *how terrible the dream is*
After this sleep of death.

> (II, pp. 377; cf. *Hamlet*, III. i. 66)

You are wanton!
Pray you, forbear. *Let me see the play.*

> (II, p. 363; cf. *Hamlet*, III. ii. 151-2)

The Unnatural Combat

It adds to my calamity, *that I have*
Discourse and reason, and but too well know

I can nor live, nor end a wretched life,
But both ways I am impious.[1]

> (I, pp. 148-9; cf. *Hamlet*, I. ii. 150-1, also
> III. viii. 36-9)

Can any penance expiate my guilt,
Or can repentance save me?[2]

> (I, p. 228; cf. *Hamlet*, III. iii. 64-6)

Thy *plurisy of goodness* is thy ill.

> (I, p. 197; cf. *Hamlet*, IV. iii. 116-7)

May the cause,
That forces me to this unnatural act
Be buried in everlasting silence,
And I find rest in death, or my revenge![3]

> (I, p. 148; cf. *Hamlet*, V. ii. 363)

JAMES SHIRLEY

The Wedding

Call this a churchyard, and imagine me
Some wakeful apparition 'mong the graves;
That, for some treasures buried in my life,
Walk up and down thus.

> (I, p. 427; cf. *Hamlet*, I. i. 136-8)

Does this inclose his corpse? *How little room*
Do we take up in death, that, living, know
No bounds? Here, without murmuring, we can
Be circumscrib'd.

> (I, p. 433; cf. *Hamlet*, V. i. 114-6)

[1] See p. 42.
[2] See p. 41.
[3] See p. 41.

1627

John Ford

'Tis Pity She's a Whore

My reason tells me now that " *'tis as common*
To err in frailty as to be a woman."
(I, p. 183; cf. Hamlet, I. ii. 146)

Nine moons have had their changes
Since I first throughly view'd and truly lov'd
Your daughter and my sister.
(I, p. 203; cf. Hamlet, III. ii. 161)

When my young *incest-monger* comes . . . let him
have your chamber and bed at liberty; let my hot hare
have law ere he be hunted to his death, that, if possible,
he may post to hell in the very act of his damnation.
(I, pp. 195-6; cf. Hamlet, III. iii. 90-5)

Philip Massinger

The Great Duke of Florence

Pray you, believe, sir,
What you deliver to me shall be *lock'd up*
In a strong cabinet, of which *you yourself*
Shall keep the key.
(II, p. 472; cf. Hamlet, I. iii. 85-6)

Well; we will clear our brows, and *undermine*
Their secret works, though they have digg'd like moles,
And crush them with the tempest of my wrath

When I appear most calm . . . They with more safety
Had trod on *fork-tongued adders*, than provoked me.
(II, pp. 483-4; cf. Hamlet, III. iv. 203-9)

1628

JOHN FORD

The Lover's Melancholy

Passions of violent nature, by degrees
Are easiliest reclaim'd. *There's something hid
Of his distemper*, which we'll now find out . . .
   [*Enter* Palador *with a book*.[1]

(I, pp. 29-30; cf. Hamlet, II. ii. 54 ff.,
also III. i. 169-70)

O, be faithful,

And let no *politic lord* work from thy bosom
My griefs: I know thou wert put on to *sift* me;
But be not too secure . . .
Continue still thy discontented fashion;
Humour the lords, as they would humour me;
I'll not live in thy debt.[2]

(I, p. 37; cf. Hamlet, II. ii. 47, 58,
also I. v. 169 ff.)

CLEOPHILA. Well, to your embassy. What, and from whom?
CUCULUS. Marry, what is more than I know; for *to know
what's what is to know what's what and for what's
what:—but these are foolish figures and to little purpose.*

(I, p. 80; cf. Hamlet, II. ii. 95-9)

[1] See p. 78.
[2] See p. 79.

> There is sense yet
> In this distraction.
>
> > (I, p. 46; cf. *Hamlet*, II. ii. 206-7)

> There is so much sense in this wild distraction,
> That I am almost out of my wits too,
> To see and hear him.
>
> > (I, p. 78; cf. *Hamlet*, II. ii. 206-7)

> Yet Athens was to me but a fair prison.
>
> > (I, p. 102; cf. *Hamlet*, II. ii. 245)

> > *Man*, the abstract
> Of all perfection, *which the workmanship*
> *Of heaven hath modell'd,*[1] in himself contains
> Passions of several qualities.
>
> > (I, p. 83; cf. *Hamlet*, II. ii. 310-14)

> > Though, by the truth
> Of love, no day hath ever pass'd wherein
> I have not mention'd thy deserts, thy constancy,
> Thy—Come, in troth, I dare not tell thee what
> *Lest thou mightst think I fawn'd on* [*thee*]—a sin
> Friendship was never guilty of; for *flattery*
> Is monstrous in a true friend.
>
> > (I, p. 12; cf. *Hamlet*, III. ii. 55-75)

> Round me, ye *guarding* ministers,
> And ever keep me waking.
>
> > (I, p. 99; cf. *Hamlet*, III. iv. 103-4)

> > In vain we strive to cross
> *The destiny that guides us.*
>
> > (I, p. 59; cf. *Hamlet*, V. ii. 10-1)

[1] See p. 77.

WILLIAM HEMINGE

The Jewes Tragedy

Be thou infernal feind confined here,
To dwell in darkness for a thousand year,
Or be thou some sad soul enforc't to dwell
Within this place, till thou return to hell,
Or *be thou Goblin, Fairy Elf or Hag,*
Or Witch in shape of wolf that lov'st to drag
Poor infants to the den; what ere thou be
If thou have power to speak, I charge thee answer me.
(ll. 1052-9; cf. Hamlet, I. iv. 40-2, also
I. i. 49)

Nay more than *seems* my friends, for *seems are show,*
But mine is substance.
(ll. 247-8; cf. Hamlet, I. ii. 76-86)

> *I can tell thee stories*
Will spurre thee on in fury to revenge.
(ll. 170-1; cf. Hamlet, I. v. 15 ff.)

GHOST. *Adiew, adiew, adiew:* expect thy doom.
(l. 2728; cf. Hamlet, I. v. 91)

Art thou there old boy?
(l. 1063; cf. Hamlet, I. v. 150)

FIRST WATCHMAN. *Where did I end* neighbour, can ye tell?
SECOND WATCHMAN. At [gate] neighbour Oliver.
(ll. 1322-3; cf. Hamlet, II. i. 51-2)

To be, or not to be, I there's the doubt.
(l. 1141; cf. Hamlet, III. i. 56)

To yeeld, or not to yeeld.

> (l. 509; cf. *Hamlet*, III. i. 56)

How my distemper'd doubts disturb my brain,
Puzzle my will, excrutiate my soul,
Distract my judgment.

> (ll. 308-10; cf. *Hamlet*, III. i. 80)

Why let the Mungril Curs go play,
And lordly Lions fight
The braver beast shall win the day,
And so my Lord good night.

> (ll. 1265-8; cf. *Hamlet*, III. ii. 276-9)

Down, down rebellious *knees;* so *stubborn* still!
I bear a burden of such massie weight
Woo'd crack the mighty Axletree of Heaven,
Yet cannot force these sturdy limbs to bend:
My Ovens mouth is damm'd with dirty sin,
No vent for sorrow; not a peeping hole
To steal a dram of comfort for my soul.

> (ll. 2412-8; cf. *Hamlet*, III. iii. 36-70)

[Zarick *hides behind the arras.*
ELEAZER. Stand close. stand close. hah. whats that.
ATTENDANT. *A ratt behinde the hangings.*

> (ll. 2801-2; cf. *Hamlet*, III. iv. 23)

Can I have brains to know, and *wil to do,*
Reason to judge, and *hands to help me too,*
And still procrastinate my daies of wo.

> (ll. 2594-6; cf. *Hamlet*, III. viii. 43-6)

Hum, hum, declare the sum of thy *concernancy*.

> (l. 1418; cf. *Hamlet*, V. ii. 124)

JAMES SHIRLEY

The Witty Fair One

I did hope, gentlemen, we should have found
My house his *bridal chamber*, not his *coffin*.
(I, p. 349; cf. *Hamlet*, V. i. 254-5)

1629

RICHARD BROME

The Northern Lasse

CONSTANCE. [*Slightly crazed from disappointment in love.*]
But *he is geane, alas hee's geane, and all too late
I sorrow:*
For I shall never be well again, till yesterday be
to-morrow.
God you good Even sir. [*Exit.*
(III, p. 53; cf. *Hamlet*, IV. i. 195-8)

Brother, I told you alwayes she had *hastie humors*, and
as unreasonable as heart can wish, *but soon over. Now
she's as mild as any Dove again.*
(III, p. 41; cf. *Hamlet*, V. i. 294-7)

JOHN FORD

The Broken Heart

She has tutor'd me;
Some powerful inspiration checks my laziness . . .
If this be madness, madness is an oracle.[1]
(I, p. 292; cf. *Hamlet*, II. ii. 206-7, also
IV. i. 176)

[1] See p. 91.

> I am thick of hearing,
> Still, *when the wind blows southerly.*
>   (I, p. 240; cf. *Hamlet*, II. ii. 387-8)

You may live well, and die a good old man:
By yea and nay, an oath not to be broken,
If you had join'd our hands once in the temple,—
'Twas since my father died, for had he liv'd
He would have done 't.[1]

                    (I, p. 293; cf. *Hamlet*, IV. i. 182-5)

THOMAS RANDOLPH

Hey For Honesty, Down With Knavery

By Jeronymo, her looks are as terrible as Don Andrea
or *the Ghost in Hamlet.*[2]

                    (II, p. 414; cf. *Hamlet*, III. iv. 124-9)

JAMES SHIRLEY

The Grateful Servant

LODOWICK. Where is he?
CLEONA. My Lord, he is gone.
LODOWICK. How?
CLEONA. *Distemper'd.*
LODOWICK. *Not with wine?*
CLEONA. Departed sick.

                    (II, p. 35; cf. *Hamlet*, III. ii. 305-10)

---

[1] See p. 90.
[2] See p. 52.

1630

WILLIAM HEMINGE

The Fatal Contract

QUEEN. [*Aside to* Landrey.] Appearing in his Brothers *war-*
    like form,[1]
    Thou wilt amaze and so passe by him safely.
    [*Aloud.*] Do not appear to me, I did not wound thee,
    Seek out the beds of those that caus'd thy death,
    And howl to them thy pittious complaints;
    O do not look on me,[2] be gone, be gone.
CLOTAIR. *Whom d'ee hold discourse with, with the air?*[3]
QUEEN. O my Son, such horrid apparitions full of dread
    Have I beheld, have quite unwitted me;
    Thy brothers Ghost, young Clovis Ghost *in armes*[4]
    Has thrice appear'd to me this dismall night . . .[5]
    [*Enter* Landrey, *as in the Princes Armour.*
CLOTAIR. *O see, it comes!*[6]
QUEEN. Fear it not, Son.
CLOTAIR. *What art thou that usurp'st this dead of night,*
    In metal like the age?[7] why art thou sent
    To cast a horror on me? *If thy soul*
    Walks unreveng'd, and the grim Ferriman
    Deny thy passage, *i'l perform thy rights.*[8]

[1] Cf. *Hamlet*, I. i. 47.   [2] Cf. *Hamlet*, III. iv. 126.
[3] Cf. *Hamlet*, III. iv. 117.   [4] Cf. *Hamlet*, I. ii. 254.
[5] Cf. *Hamlet*, I. i. 65-6.   [6] Cf. *Hamlet*, I. i. 40.
[7] Cf. *Hamlet*, I. i. 46-7.   [8] Cf. *Hamlet*, I. i. 130-1.

O do not wound me with such piteous signs.[1]
Lest I dissolve to air . . .

QUEEN. *How fares our Son?*[2]

CLOTAIR. *It was my brothers spirit . . .* [3]
This is a damned spirit I have seen,[4]
And comes to work my ruine.[5]

EUNUCH. What spirit?

CLOTAIR. *My Brothers spirit in Arms,*[6] I swear it came
forth here
Out of my Mothers Chamber as I knockt.

EUNUCH. *Was it in Armor said you?*[7]

CLOTAIR. *Yes, in that Armor he was us'd to wear*
When we have run at Tilt,[8] till our cleft Spaeres
Have with their splinters scar'd the Element.

(III. i.)

APHELIA. *Bless me Divinity,*[9] is it but a Dream! . . .

ISABEL. Did you call Maddam?

APHELIA. *Saw'st thou nothing?* . . . [10]
Methought I saw my Father[11] in a Vault . . .
Heard'st thou nothing? . . . [12]
Oh it is too true;
I 'l to my Fathers, *my Prophetique soul*[13]
Sits like a Mine of lead within me.

(IV. i. sig. G2^r-G2^v)

[1] Cf. *Hamlet*, III. iv. 127-8.
[2] Cf. *Hamlet*, III. iv. 115.
[3] Cf. *Hamlet*, I. ii. 254.
[4] Cf. *Hamlet*, III. ii. 83.
[5] Cf. *Hamlet*, II. ii. 620.
[6] Cf. *Hamlet*, I. ii. 254.
[7] Cf. *Hamlet*, I. ii. 226.
[8] Cf. *Hamlet*, I. i. 60-1.
[9] Cf. *Hamlet*, III. iv. 103-4.
[10] Cf. *Hamlet*, III. iv. 130.
[11] Cf. *Hamlet*, I. ii. 184.
[12] Cf. *Hamlet*, III. iv. 132.
[13] Cf. *Hamlet*, I. v. 40.

Are all your Troops well furnish'd 'gainst resistance?
Are your men *bold and daring, resolute*
To run your hazard, indifferent rich, not poor,
That onely fight for bread?

> (III. ii. sig. E2ᵛ; cf. *Hamlet*, I. i. 98-100)

And the discreet composure of the world
Melt and dissolve to nothing.

> (IV. i. sig. G2ᵛ; cf. *Hamlet*, I. ii. 130)

QUEEN. [*After feigning grief at her son's death.*] Did not I
     seem a Niobe in passion,
   A deluge of salt tears?

> (II. ii. sig. D4ʳ; cf. *Hamlet*, I. ii. 149)

APHELIA. If this should be dissembled, not your heart,
     And having won my souls affection,
     Should on a judgement more retir'd to state
     Smile at your perjuries, and leave me in love,
     What ill-bred tales the world would make of me?[1]

> (I. iii. sig. Cᵛ; cf. *Hamlet*, I. iii. 14-21)

APHELIA. I am too fond, and *yet he swears he loves me,*
     I have believ'd him too, for I have found
     A Godlike nature in him, and a truth
     Hitherto constant.[2]

> (I. iii. sig. Cᵛ; cf. *Hamlet*, I. iii. 110 ff.)

Plots, plots, meer fetches to delude me.[3]

> (II. i. sig. C3ᵛ; *Hamlet*, I. iii. 115)

> [*A flourish within.*

DUMAINE. Hark, the thunder of the world, how out of tune,
     This peace corrupting all things makes them speak,
     What means this most adulterate noise?

[1] See p. 46.
[2] See p. 45.
[3] See p. 45.

LAMOT. Why, are you ignorant?
This is the night of jubile, and *the King*
Solemnly feasts for his wars happie successe,
Besides his Sons and he are knit againe;
We shall have Masks and Revelling to night.
> (I. i. sig. B2ʳ-B2ᵛ; cf. *Hamlet*, I. iv. 7-12, also
> III. viii. 27)

The *Drum & Trumpet*
Sing drunken Carrols, and the *Canon speaks*
Health, not confusion; Helmets turn'd to cups.
> (I. i. sig. Bʳ; cf. *Hamlet*, I. iv. 10-12)

Unhand me Charles and render me my self,
Lest I forget my self on thee.
> (II. ii. sig. D2ʳ; cf. *Hamlet*, I. iv. 84-5)

For I am *swift as thought* that executes.
> (II. ii. sig. D2ᵛ; cf. *Hamlet*, I. v. 29-30)

I find thee Eunuch *apt* for my imployments.
> (I. ii. sig. B4ʳ; cf. *Hamlet*, I. v. 31)

I'l trouble her no further; *let her sin*
Be punish'd from above, i'l wait heavens leisure.
> (V. ii. sig. I3ᵛ; cf. *Hamlet*, I. v. 86)

O my prophetique soul.
> (II. i. sig. C4ʳ; cf. *Hamlet*, I. v. 40)

My soul finds the man, is't not Landrey?[1]
> (III. ii. sig. F4ʳ; cf. *Hamlet*, I. v. 40)

QUEEN. *Farewell, remember me.*
EUNUCH. *Remember you?*
Your Gibship shall be thought on fear it not.
> (III. ii. sig. F3ʳ; cf. *Hamlet*, I. v. 91-7)

[1] See also p. 200, note 13.

Hold, hold, my heart.
>   (II. ii. sig. D2^r; cf. *Hamlet*, I. v. 93)

Hold my heart.
>   (IV. i. sig. G^v; cf. *Hamlet*, I. v. 93)

Hold my heart.
>   (IV. iii. sig. H^v; cf. *Hamlet*, I. v. 93)

Hold, hold, my heart.
>   (V. ii. sig. K^v; cf. *Hamlet*, I. v. 93)

>   My *brains* grow weak;
And in this Globe *the policie's* not left
To kill a worm unseen.
>   (III. ii. sig. F2^v; cf. *Hamlet*, II. ii. 46-7)

He is in love that's certain; let me remember,
When I was first a lover as he is,
I'd just such wild vagaries in my brain,
Such midnight madness; this puling baggage
May lose her self for ever, and her fortunes,
By this hours absence.[1]

>   (II. i. sig. C.4^r-C4^v; cf. *Hamlet*, II. ii. 189-91,
>   also II. i. 102 ff.)

Then Dooms-day is at hand.
>   (V. ii. sig. I3^v; cf. *Hamlet*, II. ii. 240)

As a good Actor in a play would do,
Whose fancy works (as if he waking dreamt)
Too strongly on the Object that it copes with,
Shaping realities from mockeries;
And so the queen *did weep.*

>   (II. ii. sig. D4^r; cf. *Hamlet*, II, ii. 565 ff.)

[1] See p. 46.

About my brain.
> (III. i. sig. E2^v; cf. *Hamlet*, II. ii. 605)

The Devill can assume an Angels form.
> (IV. i. sig. G^v; cf. *Hamlet*, II. ii. 616-7)

KING. [*Interrupting the masque.*] Defer our pastimes till another night,
I am not well at ease.
DUMAINE. *Lights, lights for his Majesty.*
CLOTAIR and CLOVIS. *How is it with your grace* our Royal Father?
> (I. iii. sig. C2^v; cf. *Hamlet*, III. ii. 270-5)

By this good night
I think I could become the Stage as well
As any she that sels her breath in publique.
> (II. ii. sig. D4^r; cf. *Hamlet*, III. ii. 280-4)

I 'l take thy word Eunuch *for the Kingdoms wealth.*
> (IV. ii. sig. G3^r; cf. *Hamlet*, III. ii. 292-3)

What French *Neronian spirit* have we here?
> (IV. iii. sig. H2^r; cf. *Hamlet*, III. iii. 404)

If (in her proud desire) *I do prevent*
Her lust this second time, before the third
She may repent and save her loathed soul,
Which my revenge would damn; yet were she crost,
Her lust being now at full flood within her,
And no way left to quench her burning flame,
Her dryer bones would make a bonfire,
Fit for the Devill to warm his hands by.
> (III. ii. sig. F3^r; cf. *Hamlet*, III. iii. 89-95)

CLOVIS. O that I had no eyes, so you no shame;
    Murther your Husband to arrive at lust,
    And then to lay the blame on innocents?
    Blush, blush, thou worse than woman.
QUEEN. How dar'st thou cloth thy speech in such a phrase
    To me *thy naturall mother?*
CLOVIS. My mother!
    Adulterate woman, *shame of Royaltie*
    I blush to call thee mother; thy foul lusts
    Have taught me words of that harsh consequence
    That Stigmatize obedience, *and do brand*
    With mis-becoming accents filiall duty.[1]

         (IV. iii. sig. H^v; cf. *Hamlet*, III. iv. 14 ff.)

    Into thy bosome cast thine inward eyes,
    And view the sorrows I have heaped on thee.
         (V. ii. sig. K^r; cf. *Hamlet*, III. iv. 89-90)

QUEEN. [*As her son enters in his murdered father's robes.*]
    Guard me divinitie.
         (IV. ii. sig. G4^v; cf. *Hamlet*, III. iv. 104-5)

         Flie me not,
  I am no spirit: *tast my active pulse,*
  And you shall find it make such harmony,
  As youth and health enjoy.
         (III. ii. sig. F^r; cf. *Hamlet*, III. iv. 140-1)

I 'l *set them packing*, fear not.
         (IV. iii. sig. H2^r; cf. *Hamlet*, III, iv. 211)

         The no chast Queene,
  Is as her birth, as great in faction,

[1] See p. 44.

Followed and sainted by the multitude,
Whose judgement she hath linck'd unto her Purse.[1]
> (I. i. sig. B2ʳ; cf. *Hamlet*, III. vii. 3-5)

> *As thy King*
Divinity doth prop him, he stands firm
That builds on that foundation.
> (II. ii. sig. D3ʳ; cf. *Hamlet*, IV. i. 122-4)

So Centaur-like *he 's anckor'd to his seat,*
As he had twind with the proud steed he rides on;
He grows unto his saddle all one piece,
And that unto his Horse.
> (V. ii. sig. I3ʳ; cf. *Hamlet*, IV. iii. 84-7)

King, thou hadst better far have strook thy Father,
Dig'd up his bones and plaid at logats with them.
> (III. i. sig. E2ʳ; cf. *Hamlet*, V. i. 94-5)

A hopeful *youth, fraught with Nobility,*
And all the graceful qualities that write
Man truly honourable.[2]
> (IV. iii. sig. H2ʳ; cf. *Hamlet*, V. i. 233-4)

There lies a depth in fate, which earthly eies
May faintly look into, but cannot fathom.
> (III. ii. sig. F2ʳ; cf. *Hamlet*, V. ii. 10-11)

Behold my Lord, *the Woodcock 's in the Gin,*
Here lies the great Landrey.
> (IV. iii. sig. H2ʳ; cf. *Hamlet*, V. ii. 311)

There's not an hours life between ye both;
The poyson's sure, I did prepare it for ye.
> (V. ii. sig. H4ᵛ; cf. *Hamlet*, V. ii. 320-2)

[1] See p. 43.
[2] See p. 47.

CLOTAIR. [*Dying.*] Good gentle souls when ye shal mention
    me,
  And elder time shall rip these stories up,
  Dissected and Anatomiz'd by you;
  Touch sparingly this story, do not read
  Too harsh a comment on this loathed deed,
  Lest you inforce posterity to blast
  My name and Memory with endless curses.[1]
        (V. ii. sig. K2ᵛ; cf. *Hamlet*, V. ii. 343 ff.)

THOMAS RANDOLPH

The Muses' Looking-Glass

TRAGEDY. But I move horror, and that *frights the guilty*
  From his dear sins . . .
  Who will rely on *fortune's giddy smile*,
  That hath seen *Priam acted on the stage?*
      (I, p. 188; cf. *Hamlet*, II. ii. 504-9, 578, 606 ff.)

  It is the *whirlwind* of the soul, the storm
  And *tempest* of the mind, that raises up
  The billows of disturbed *passions*
  To shipwreck judgment.
        (I, p. 230; cf. *Hamlet*, III. ii. 5-7)

  So *comedies*, as poets do intend them,
  Serve first to show our faults, and then to mend them.
  Upon our stage two glasses oft there be;
  The comic mirror and the tragedy:
  The *comic glass* is full of merry strife,
  The low *reflection* of a country life.
  Grave tragedy, void of such homely sports,
  Is the *sad glass* of cities and of courts.
        (I, p. 186; cf. *Hamlet*, III. ii. 21-6)

[1] See p. 47.

1631

Philip Massinger

Believe As You List

And room enough
To tumble in, I pray you, *though I take up
More grave than Alexander.* I have ill luck
If I stink not as much as he, and yield the worms
As large a supper.

(p. 619; cf. *Hamlet*, V. i. 206-26)

The Emperor of the East

My prophetic soul.

(III, p. 266; cf. *Hamlet*, I. v. 40)

I was lost
In my astonishment at the glorious object,
And yet rest doubtful whether he expects,
Being more than man, my adoration,
Since sure *there is divinity about him.*

(III, p. 282; cf. *Hamlet*, IV. i. 122-4)

James Shirley

Honoria and Mammon

What a base *prison* to a noble soul
The world is.

(VI, p. 49; cf. *Hamlet*, II. ii. 246)

The Traitor

DUKE. Oh, spare me; I may live, and pardon thee:
    Thy prince begs mercy from thee, that did never

Deny thee any thing; *pity my poor soul;*
I have not pray'd.
LORENZO. I could have wish'd you better
Prepar'd, but *let your soul e'en take his chance.*
                    (II, p. 183; cf. *Hamlet*, III. iii. 89-95)

DEPAZZI. Sirrah, sirrah, sirrah, *I smell a rat behind the hang-*
ings. [*Takes up the hangings.*] Here's no body.
                    (II, p. 129; cf. *Hamlet*, III. iv. 24)

Where's the duke? *he hath a guard,*
An army of heaven about him; who in Florence
Dares be so black a devil to attempt
His death?

(II, p. 146; cf. *Hamlet*, IV. i. 122-4)

1632

RICHARD BROME

The Court Beggar

Embrace
The hopes that I have for thee in the hopefull,
Exquisite Cavalier, *Courtier and Souldier,*
Scholler . . . brave Sir Ferdinando.
                    (I, p. 186; cf. *Hamlet*, III. i. 156)

Heape yet more Mountaines, Mountaines upon
Mountaines, Pindus on Ossa, Atlas on Olympus,
I'le carry that which carries Heaven, do you
But lay't upon me!

(I, p. 245; cf. *Hamlet*, V. i. 289-92)

Thomas Heywood

The English Traveller

My braine, about it then.

> (IV, p. 37; cf. *Hamlet*, II. ii. 605)

WIFE. To whom speakes the man?
GERALDINE.   To thee,
  Falsest of all that ever man term'd faire;
  Hath Impudence so steel'd thy smooth soft skin,
  It cannot blush? Or sinne so obdur'd thy heart,
  It does not quake and tremble.

> (IV, p. 90; cf. *Hamlet*, III. iv. 35-8, 82)

Ben Jonson

The Magnetic Lady

The *courtiers,* and the *soldiers,* and the *scholars.*

> (VI, p. 18; cf. *Hamlet*, III. i. 156)

If I see a thing vively presented on the *stage,* that *the glass of custom, which is comedy, is so held up to me by the poet, as I can therein view the daily examples of men's lives, and images of truth, in their manners, so drawn for my delight or profit, as I may,* either way, use them.

> (VI, pp. 47-8; cf. *Hamlet*, III. ii. 21-6)

Thomas Middleton

The Changeling

O my presaging soul!

> (V. i. 108; cf. *Hamlet*, I. v. 40)

ALSEMERO. Pray, resolve me one question, lady.
BEATRICE. If I can.
ALSEMERO. None can so sure: *are you honest?*
BEATRICE. Ha, ha, ha! that's a broad question, my lord.
(V. iii. 20-2; cf. Hamlet, III. i. 103-6)

Earth-conquering Alexander, that thought the world
Too narrow for him, in th' end had but his pit-hole.
(IV. i. 63-4; cf. Hamlet, V. i. 206-21)

THOMAS NABBES

Covent Garden

DOROTHY. Hath not *feare* congeal'd them into stones?
SUSAN. *Dissolv'd them rather into gelley.*
(I, p. 43; cf. Hamlet, I. ii. 204-5)

THOMAS RANDOLPH

The Jealous Lovers

When I sleep

Within my quiet grave, I shall have dreams.
(I, p. 71; cf. Hamlet, III. i. 65-6)

Now, my sword,

That hadst a good edge to defend this woman,
Go send her soul into another mansion,
Black as itself. It is too foul a tenant
For this fair place. *Stay yet, too forward steel:*
Take her encircled in her stallion's arms,
And kill two sins together. Let 'em be
At hell to bear the punishment of lust,
Ere it be fully acted.
(I, p. 128; cf. Hamlet, III. iii. 90-5)

And is it possible so divine a goddess
Should fall from heaven to wallow here in sin
With a baboon as this is?
>   (I, p. 81; cf. *Hamlet*, III. iv. 66-71)

>   You shall be milked,
Emptied and pump'd. *Sponge, we will squeeze you,
sponge,*
And send you to suck more.
>   (I, p. 121; cf. *Hamlet*, III. vi. 14-21)

This was a captain's skull, one that carried a storm in
his countenance and a tempest in his tongue; the great
bugbear of the city, that threw drawers down the stairs
as familiarly as quart-pots; and had a pension from
the barber-chirurgeons for breaking of pates: a fellow
that had ruined the noses of more bawds and panders
than the disease belonging to the trade; and yet I
remember, when he went to burial, another corse
took the wall of him, and the bandog ne'er grum-
bled.[1]
>   (I, p. 139; cf. *Hamlet*, V. i. 81 ff.)

This was a poetical noddle. O, the sweet lines, choice
language, eloquent figures, besides the jests, half-jests,
quarter-jests, and quibbles that have come out o' these
chaps that yawn so! He has not now so much as a
new-coined compliment to procure him a supper. The
best friend he has may walk by him now, and yet have
ne'er a jeer put upon him. His mistress had a little dog
deceased the other day, and all the wit in this noddle
could not pump out an elegy to bewail it. He has been
my tenant these seven years, and in all that while I

[1] See p. 112.

never heard him rail against the times, or complain of
the neglect of learning.[1]

(I, p. 140; cf. Hamlet, V. i. 81 ff.)

Look here! *this is a lawyer's skull.* There was a tongue
in 't once, a damnable eloquent tongue, that would almost have persuaded any man to the gallows. This was
a turbulent, busy fellow, till death gave him his *quietus
est.* And yet I ventured to rob him of his gown and
the rest of his habiliments, to the very buckram
bag . . . [*To the skull.*] *Now a man may clap you o'
th' coxcomb with his spade, and never stand in fear
of an action of battery.*[2]

(I, pp. 143-4; cf. Hamlet, V. i. 101-6, also
III. i. 75)

This was the prime madam in Thebes, the general mistress, the only adored beauty. Little would you think
there were a couple of ears in these two auger-holes:
or that this pit had been arched over with a handsome
nose, that had been at the charges to maintain half a
dozen of several silver arches to uphold the bridge.
*It had been a mighty favour once to have kissed these
lips that grin so.* This mouth out of all the madam's
boxes cannot now be furnished with a set of teeth. She
was the coyest, [most] overcurious dame in all the city:
her chambermaid's misplacing of a hair was as much as
her place came to. *O, if that lady now could but behold this physnomy of hers in a looking-glass, what a
monster would she imagine herself!* Will all her perukes, tires, and dresses; with her chargeable teeth, with
her ceruse and pomatum, and *the benefit of her painter*
and doctor, make this idol up again?

[1] See p. 113.
[2] See p. 114.

Paint, ladies, while you live, and plaister fair;
But when the house is fallen, 'tis past repair.[1]

(I, p. 141; cf. *Hamlet*, V. i. 196-204)

1633

JAMES SHIRLEY

The Young Admiral

My prophetic soul
Knew this before.

(III, p. 111; cf. *Hamlet*, I. v. 40)

1634

THOMAS HEYWOOD

Love's Mistress

Of Vulcans Ciclopps Ile so much intreate,
That thou shalt see them on their Anvile beate;
'Tis musicke fitting thee, for who but knowes,
The Vulgar are best pleas'd with noyse and showes?

(V, p. 146; cf. *Hamlet*, III. ii. 10-12)

PHILIP MASSINGER

A Very Woman

She 's constant—*but a woman;*
And what a lover's vows, persuasions, tears,
May, in a minute, work upon *such frailty,*
There are too many and too sad examples.

(IV, p. 249; cf. *Hamlet*, I. ii. 146)

[1] See pp. 113-14.

MERCHANT. Now observe him nearly.
[*The English Slave practices his postures.*
PAULO. *This fellow's mad, stark mad.*
MERCHANT. *Believe they are all so:*
    I have sold a hundred of them.
PAULO. A strange nation!
    What may the women be?
MERCHANT. As mad as they,
    And, as I have heard for truth, a great deal madder:
    Yet, you may find some civil things amongst them,
    But they are not respected.
                    (IV, p. 285; cf. *Hamlet*, V. i. 156-62)

J. RUTTER

The Shepherd's Holiday

                    What are you?
Came you from heaven, where my Sylvia is,
And must I thither? whosoe'er you are,
An angel or a fiend, in such a name
You come, as I 'm conjur'd to follow you.
            (Dodsley's *Old English Plays* ed. by W. C.
            Hazlitt, XII, p. 411; cf. *Hamlet*, I. iv. 40-4)

JAMES SHIRLEY

Love Tricks

Old men walk with a staff, and creep along the street,
hold their heads below their girdle, faulter in their
speech, foam at the mouth, breathe ten times in a fur-
long, and are ready to spit their lungs on every man's
threshold.

            (I, p. 13; cf. *Hamlet*, II. ii. 198-201)

1635

Richard Brome

The Queen and the Concubine

horatio. *Look there, the Apparition, there it is;*
    As like the Traytor Sforza when he liv'd.
                    (II, p. 104; cf. *Hamlet*, I. i. 40-1)

No, we will make such a Reformation, that *Treason*
shall not dare to peep over the Hedge of her Dominion,
but we will take it by the nose and punish it indignely.
                    (II, p. 116; cf. *Hamlet*, IV. i. 122-4)

Henry Glapthorne

The Lady Mother

The glowewormes ineffectual fire.
    (*Old English Plays* ed. by A. H. Bullen, II, p. 178;
    cf. *Hamlet*, I. v. 90)

Shakerly Marmion

The Antiquary

Look, where the ghost appears, his wounds fresh-bleed-
    ing!
He frowns and threatens me . . .
Do not stare so . . .
Now he vanishes;
Dost thou *steal* from me, fearful spirit? See
The print of his footsteps!
    (Dodsley's *Old English Plays* ed. by W. C. Hazlitt,
    XIII, p. 513; cf. *Hamlet*, I. i. 40, also III. iv. 124-35)

Thomas Nabbes

Hannibal and Scipio

My sad *soule*
Labours with a *prophetick* apprehension.
(I, p. 263; cf. *Hamlet*, I. v. 40)

1637

John Suckling

Aglaura

What wretch is this that thus *usurps*
Upon the privilege of ghosts, *and walks*
At midnight?
(III. ii. 2-4; cf. *Hamlet*, I. i. 46)

That, do we what we can, we are not able
Without cold meats to furnish out the table.
(Epilogue to Act V as presented at Court;
cf. *Hamlet*, I. ii. 180-1)

Down, sorrow, down,
And swell my heart no more! *and thou, wrong'd ghost*
Of my dead father, to thy bed again,
And sleep securely![1]
(I. ii. 25-8; cf. *Hamlet*, I. v. 182)

Some *devil*, sure, has borrowed *this shape.*
(V. i. 54; cf. *Hamlet*, II. ii. 616-7)

[1] See p. 49.

For ever? Ay, there's it!
For in those groves thou talk'st of,
There are so many byways and odd turnings,
Leading unto such wide and dismal places,
That should we go without a guide, or stir
Before heav'n calls, 'tis strongly to be feared,
We there should wander up and down for ever,
And be benighted to eternity.[1]
                (V. ii. 56-63; cf. *Hamlet*, III. i. 65 ff.)

If to be free from the *great load we sweat*
And labour under here on earth, be to
Be well, he is.[2]
                (V. iii. 28-30; cf. *Hamlet*, III. i. 76-7)

If to be on's *journey to the other world*
Be to be well, he is.[3]
                (V. iii. 16-17 as presented at Court; cf. *Hamlet*,
                III. i. 79-80)

Hope on his future fortunes, or their love
Unto his person, *has so sicklied o'er*
Their resolutions, that we must not trust them.
                (IV. i. 56-8; cf. *Hamlet*, III. i. 84-5)

For in my thoughts and here within I hold her
The noblest piece *Nature* e'er lent our eyes,
And of the which all women else are but
Weak counterfeits, made up by her journeymen.
                (II. i. 22-5; cf. *Hamlet*, III. ii. 34-6)

[1] See pp. 49-50.
[2] See p. 50.
[3] See p. 50, note 2.

What a strange *glass th' have showed me now myself*
in!

> (V. iv. 93 as presented at Court; cf. *Hamlet*,
> III. iv. 19-20)

Like a *distracted multitude.*

> (V. ii. 17; cf. *Hamlet*, III. vii. 4)

> For to thy memory
Such tribute of moist sorrow I will pay,
And that so purifi'd by love, that *on*
Thy grave nothing shall grow but violets
And primroses.

> (V. iii. 150-4; cf. *Hamlet*, V. i. 248-9)

> *The hopes of all my youth,*
And a reward which Heav'n hath settled on me
(If holy contracts can do anything)
He ravish'd from me, kill'd my father—
Aglaura's father, sir—*would have whor'd my sister*
And murthered my friend.[1]

> (V. iv. 80-5 as presented at Court; cf.
> *Hamlet*, V. ii. 64-7)

The Sad One

Fain would I make *my audit up with heaven.*

> (I. i. 37; cf. *Hamlet*, III. iii. 82)

> So, my revenge
Flies high: the villain first shall kill his father;
And, *while his hands are hot i' th' blood, this sword*
Shall pierce him. Murder'd he shall sink quick to hell:
I will not give him leave t' unload himself
Of one poor single sin of thought.

> (II. v. 10-15; cf. *Hamlet*, III. iii. 89-95)

[1] See p. 48.

1638

RICHARD BROME

The Antipodes

LETOY. Trouble not your head with my conceite,
　But mind your part. Let me not see you act now,
　In your Scholasticke way, you brought to towne
　　wi' yee,
　With see saw sacke a downe, like a Sawyer;
　Nor in a Comicke Scene, play Hercules furens,
　Tearing your throat to split the Audients eares.
　And you Sir, you had got a tricke of late,
　Of holding out your bum in a set speech;
　Your fingers fibulating on your breast,
　As if your Buttons, or your Band-strings were
　Helpes to your memory. Let me see you in 't
　No more I charge you. No, nor you sir, in
　That over-action of the legges I told you of,
　Your singles, and your doubles, Looke you—thus—
　Like one o' th' dancing Masters o' the Beare-garden;
　And when you have spoke, at end of every speech,
　Not minding the reply, you turne you round
　As Tumblers doe; when betwixt every feat
　They gather wind, by firking up their breeches.
　Ile none of these, absurdities in my house.
　But words and action married so together,
　That shall strike harmony in the eares and eyes
　Of the severest, if judicious Criticks.
QUAILE-PIPE. *My lord we are corrected.*
LETOY. *Goe, be ready:* [*Turning to the Clown.*
　But you Sir are incorrigible, and
　Take licence to your selfe, to adde unto
　Your parts, your owne free fancy; and sometimes

To alter, or diminish what the writer
With care and skill compos'd: and when you are
To speak to your coactors in the Scene,
You hold interloquutions with the Audients.
BIPLAY. That is a way my Lord has bin allow'd
   On elder stages to move mirth and laughter.
LETOY. Yes in the dayes of Tarlton and Kempe,
   Before the stage was purg'd from barbarisme,
   And brought to the perfection it now shines with.
   Then fooles and jesters spent their wits, because
   The Poets were wise enough to save their owne
   For profitabler uses.[1]

(III, pp. 259-60; cf. Hamlet, III. ii. 4 ff.)

The Damoiselle

Full six and thirty times hath Luna wan'd
The strength she got in six and thirty growths
From Phoebus vertuous beames, into this Juyce,
To make it Nectar for Phoebean wits.

(I, p. 421; cf. Hamlet, III. ii. 159-62)

JAMES SHIRLEY

The Constant Maid

The herbs that shall *adorn your bridal chamber*
Will serve my funeral, and *deck my herse.*

(IV, p. 503; cf. Hamlet, V. i. 254-5)

The Royal Master

DOMITILLA. I know not how I may
   Stand guilty in your thoughts, by keeping a
   Rich carcanet.
DUKE. You honour'd me to accept it . . .

[1] See pp. 100-1.

Madam, it is not worth
The mention of this gratitude; *your breath*
Makes the oblation rich.

(IV, pp. 173-4; cf. *Hamlet*, III. i. 98-9)

KING. *Are you honest?*
THEODOSIA. Honest!
KING. I could have us'd the name of chaste,
  Or virgin; but they carry the same sense.

(IV, p. 156; cf. *Hamlet*, III. i. 103)

JOHN SUCKLING

The Goblins

The secret of the prison-house
Shall out, I swear.

(V. i. 41-2; cf. *Hamlet*, I. v. 14)

Well, I must resolve;
But what, or where? *Ay, that's the question.*

(IV. v. 8-9; cf. *Hamlet*, III. i. 56)

To die! Ay, what's that?
For yet I never thought on 't seriously.
It may be 'tis—hum!—it may be 'tis not, too.

(III. iii. 1-3; cf. *Hamlet*, III. i. 60)

1639

THOMAS NABBES

The Unfortunate Mother

Y' are a Prince
And *every act of yours concernes a state,*
Not your meere person onely: what you doe

Must therefore deeply be consider'd on . . .
Princes should wed with Princesse.[1]
> (*Old English Plays, New Series*, ed. by A. H. Bullen,
> II, p. 98; cf. *Hamlet*, I. iii. 16 ff.)

CORVINO. [*Referring to his daughter* Melissa, *whom he
wishes to prevent from marriage with* Fidelio.]
Give me a fathers priviledge to prepare her
With *some fit precepts* . . .
> [*A few minutes later to* Melissa.
I 'ld have you quench that low and common flame
That burnes towards Fidelio; and embrace
Those high desires I point you to: *my pollicy
Hath order'd the successe.*
> (*Ibid.*, II, p. 141; cf. *Hamlet*, II. ii. 47, 142 ff.)

Did *my election from a world of men*
Single thee out to be so much my selfe;
The union of our *soules* would not admit
Of a division, but that interchange
And custome taught us read each others thoughts?
> (*Ibid.*, II, p. 135; cf. *Hamlet*, III. ii. 64-6)

JOHN SUCKLING

The Tragedy of Brennoralt

Pish, 'tis mere fondness in our nature,
A certain clownish cowardice, that still
Would stay at home, *and dares not venture into
Foreign countries*, though better than its own!
Ha, what countries? for we receive descriptions
Of th' other world from our divines, as blind
Men take relation of this from us.
> (II. i. 14-20; cf. *Hamlet*, III. i. 76-83)

[1] See p. 97.

ALMERIN. [*Dying.*] Stay, thou much-wearied guest,
Till I have thrown a truth amongst them—
We shall look black else to posterity.
                    (V. iii. 98-100; cf. *Hamlet*, V. ii. 349-54)

1640

RICHARD BROME

The Lovesick Court

Let not the royal blood
Of Thessaly be stain'd with an *incestuous* match.
                    (II, p. 166; cf. *Hamlet*, I. v. 82-3)

GEORGE CHAPMAN (?)

Revenge For Honour

CAROPIA. The dead Prince sends you that. [*Stabs him.*
MURA. O, I am slain!
CAROPIA.   *Would it were possible*
To kill even thy eternity!
                    (IV. ii. 64-6; cf. *Hamlet*, III. iii. 89-95)

JAMES SHIRLEY

The Arcadia

What *prophetic soul.*
                    (VI, p. 216; cf. *Hamlet*, I. v. 40)

The Doubtful Heir

                    Live thou, oh live!
And if thou hast a tear, when I am dead,
But drop it to my memory . . .

There will be none to speak of Ferdinand
Without disdain, if thou diest too. Oh, live
A little, to defend me, or, at least,
To say I was no traitor to thy love;
And lay the shame on death, and my false stars,
That would not let me live to be a king.

(IV, pp. 301-2; cf. *Hamlet*, V. ii. 343 ff.)

1641

JAMES SHIRLEY

The Cardinal

CARDINAL. It troubles me the duchess, by her loss
Of brain, is now beneath my great revenge . . .
I shall lose by killing her,
Perhaps do her a pleasure and preferment . . .
'Tis too cheap
A satisfaction for Columbo's death,
Only to kill her by soft charm or force.
I'll rifle first her darling chastity;
It will be after time enough *to poison her.*

(V, pp. 333-5; cf. *Hamlet*, III. iii. 76-95)

Later in the play:

KING. How came you by that poison?
CARDINAL.   I prepar'd it,
   Resolving, when I had enjoy'd her, which
   The colonel prevented, *by some art*
   To make her take it, and by death conclude
   My last revenge.

(V, p. 350; cf. *Hamlet*, III. iii. 90-5)

But, if I were to kill him, *he should have*
No time to pray; his life could be no sacrifice,
Unless his soul went too.

(V, p. 316; cf. *Hamlet*, III. iii. 93-5)

1642

JAMES SHIRLEY

The Court Secret

My *soul* has been a *prophet*.

(V, p. 491; cf. *Hamlet*, I. v. 40)

Why should we murmur to be circumscrib'd,
As if it were a new thing to wear fetters,
When the whole world was meant but to confine us;
Wherein who walks from one clime to another,
Hath but a greater freedom of the prison?

(V, p. 460; cf. *Hamlet*, II. ii. 245-7)

MENDOZA. I would *thou wert shipp'd.*
PEDRO. And sunk.—
    It shall go hard but I'll requite your lordship.

(V, p. 456; cf. *Hamlet*, III. iv. 207-8)

BIBLIOGRAPHY

A., R., Gent. *The Valiant Welshman* ed. by Valentin Kreb. Erlangen and Leipzig, 1902. (*Münchener Beiträge zur Romanischen und Englischen Philologie*, XXIII)

Adams, Joseph Q. *A Life of William Shakespeare.* Boston and New York, 1923.

Adams, Joseph Q. "William Heminge and Shakespeare." *Modern Philology*, XII, pp. 51-64, May, 1914.

Alden, R. M. *The Rise of Formal Satire in England under Classical Influence.* Philadelphia, 1899. (*Publications of the University of Pennsylvania. Series in Philology, Literature, and Archaeology*, VII, 2)

Armin, Robert. *Works . . .* ed. by A. B. Grosart. Manchester, 1880. (*Occasional Issues of Unique or Very Rare Books*, XIV)

Beaumont and Fletcher. *The Works of Francis Beaumont and John Fletcher* ed. by A. Glover and A. R. Waller. Cambridge, 1905-12. 10 v.

Brome, Richard. *Dramatic Works.* London, 1873. 3 v.

Bullen, A. H. *A Collection of Old English Plays* ed. by A. H. Bullen. London, 1882-85. 4 v.

Bullen, A. H. *Old English Plays, New Series,* ed. by A. H. Bullen. London, 1887-90. 3 v.

The Cambridge History of English Literature ed. by A. W. Ward and A. R. Waller. New York and London, 1907-17. v-vi.

Chambers, E. K. *The Elizabethan Stage*. Oxford, 1923. 4 v.

Chambers, E. K. *William Shakespeare: A Study of Facts and Problems*. Oxford, 1930. 2 v.

Chapman, George. *Plays and Poems* ed. by T. M. Parrott. London and New York, 1910-14. 2 v.

Chettle, Henry. *The Tragedy of Hoffman, or a Revenge for a Father* ed. by Richard Ackermann. Bamberg, 1894.

D'Avenant, William. *Dramatic Works*. Edinburgh, 1872-74. 5 v. (*Dramatists of the Restoration, D'Avenant*)

Day, John. *Works* ed. by A. H. Bullen. London, 1881. 2 v.

Dekker, Thomas. *Dramatic Works*. London, 1873. (Pearson's Reprint)

Ford, John. *Works* ed. by W. Gifford and A. Dyce. London, 1895. 3 v.

Glapthorne, Henry. *Plays and Poems*. London, 1874. 2 v. (Pearson's Reprint)

Glapthorne, Henry. *The Lady Mother*. (In Bullen, A. H., ed., *A Collection of Old English Plays*. London, 1882-85, II, pp. 101-200)

Harbage, Alfred. *Cavalier Drama; An Historical and Critical Supplement to the Study of the Elizabethan and Restoration Stage*. New York and London, 1936.

Hazlitt, W. C. *A Select Collection of Old English Plays. Originally Published by Robert Dodsley in the year 1744*. London, 1874-75. VIII-XIV.

Heminge, William. *The Fatal Contract*. London, 1653.

Heminge, William. *The Jewes Tragedy von William*

Hemings ed. by H. A. Cohn. Louvain, 1913. (*Materialien zur Kunde des älteren Englischen Dramas*, XL)

Heywood, Thomas. *Dramatic Works*. London, 1874. 6 v. (Pearson's Reprint)

Heywood, Thomas. *The Captives; or, the Lost Recovered* ed. by A. C. Judson. New Haven, 1921.

Jonson, Ben. *Ben Jonson* ed. by C. H. Herford and Percy Simpson. Oxford, 1925- .

Jonson, Ben. *The Works of Ben Jonson* ed. by W. Gifford and F. Cunningham. London, 1875. 9 v.

Marston, John. *Works* ed. by A. H. Bullen. London and Boston, 1887. 3 v.

Marston, John. *Plays* ed. by H. Harvey Wood. Edinburgh, 1934- .

Massinger, Philip. *Plays* ed. by W. Gifford. London, 1813. 4 v.

Massinger, Philip. *Believe as You List* ed. by F. Cunningham. London, 1868.

Middleton, Thomas. *Works* ed. by A. H. Bullen. London, 1885-86. 8 v.

Munro, John. *The Shakspere Allusion-Book: a Collection of Allusions to Shakspere from 1591 to 1700*. Originally compiled by C. M. Ingleby, Miss L. Toulmin Smith, and Dr. F. J. Furnivall, with the assistance of the New Shakspere society; and now re-edited, revised, and re-arranged, with an introduction, by John Munro. London and New York, 1909. 2 v. (*The Shakespeare Library* ed. by Prof. I. Gollancz)

Nabbes, Thomas. *Works*. (In Bullen, A. H., ed., *Old English Plays, New Series*. London, 1887-90. I-II)

The Oxford Dictionary of English Proverbs. Compiled by William G. Smith . . . and Janet E. Haseltine. Oxford, 1935.

Patient Grissil: a Comedy by Thomas Dekker, Henry Chettle, and William Haughton. London, Printed for the Shakespeare society, 1841.

Randolph, Thomas. *Poetical and Dramatic Works* ed. by W. C. Hazlitt. London, 1875. 2 v.

Raven, Anton A. *A Hamlet Bibliography and Reference Guide.* Chicago, 1936.

Rowley, William. *A Match at Midnight.* (In Dodsley's *A Select Collection of Old English Plays* ed. by W. C. Hazlitt, VII)

Rowley, William. *William Rowley, his All's Lost by Lust and a Shoemaker, a Gentleman* ed. by C. W. Stork. Philadelphia, 1910. (*Publications of the University of Pennsylvania, Series in Philology and Literature,* XIII)

Rowley, William. *The Birth of Merlin* ed. by K. Warnke and L. Proescholdt. Halle, 1887. (*Pseudo-Shakespearean Plays,* IV)

Schelling, F. E. *Elizabethan Drama 1558-1642.* Boston and New York, 1908. 2 v.

Shakespeare, William. *Hamlet Prince of Denmark* ed. by Joseph Q. Adams. New York, 1929. (All references to *Hamlet* in this study are to this edition.)

Shakespeare, William. *Hamlet* ed. by J. Dover Wilson. Cambridge, 1934.

Shirley, James. *Dramatic Works and Poems* ed. by W. Gifford and A. Dyce. London, 1833. 6 v.

Suckling, John. *Works . . . in Prose and Verse* ed. by A. H. Thompson. London, 1910.

Swetnam the Woman Hater Arraigned by Women ed. by A. B. Grosart. Manchester, 1880. (*Occasional Issues of Unique or Very Rare Books*, XIV)

Thorndike, A. H. "The Relations of *Hamlet* to Contemporary Revenge Plays." *PMLA*, XVII, pp. 125-220, 1902.

Tourneur, Cyril. *The Atheist's Tragedy, or the Honest Man's Revenge* ed. by J. A. Symonds. London, 1888. (In *The Mermaid Series, The Best Plays of the Old Dramatists, Webster and Tourneur*)

Tourneur, Cyril. *The Revenger's Tragedy* ed. by J. A. Symonds. London, 1888. (In *The Mermaid Series, The Best Plays of the Old Dramatists, Webster and Tourneur*)

Webster, John. *Works* ed. by F. J. Lucas. London, 1927. 4 v.

Wilson, J. Dover. *What Happens in Hamlet.* New York, 1935.

INDEX